INNOVATIVE MINDS

GEORGE WESTINGHOUSE

A GENIUS FOR INVENTION

Barbara Ravage

Austin, Texas

To my son, JC, whose interest in trains kept me going, and to Garry Meyers, who taught me everything I know about putting words together.

Acknowledgements
The author and publisher would like to acknowledge Mr. Charlie Ruch, company historian for the Westinghouse Electric Corporation, for his help in securing photos and his expert review of the manuscript.

Published by Raintree Steck-Vaughn Publishers, an imprint of Steck-Vaughn Company.

Series created by Blackbirch Graphics
Series Editor: Tanya Lee Stone
Editor: Lisa Clyde Nielsen
Associate Editor: Elizabeth M. Taylor
Production/Design Editor: Calico Harington

Raintree Steck-Vaughn Staff
Editors: Shirley Shalit, Kathy DeVico
Project Manager: Lyda Guz

Library of Congress Cataloging-in-Publication Data

Ravage, Barbara.
George Westinghouse: a genius for invention / by Barbara Ravage.
p. cm. — (Innovative minds)
Includes bibliographical references and index.
Summary: Examines the life and work of the determined, forward-thinking inventor, who held more than three hundred patents by the time he died.
ISBN 0-8172-4402-6
1. Westinghouse, George, 1846–1914—Juvenile. 2. Inventors—United States—Biography—Juvenile literature. [1. Westinghouse, George, 1846–1914. 2. Inventors.] I. Title. II. Series.
T40.W4R38 1997
620'.0092—dc20 96-17490
[B] CIP
AC

Printed in the United States of America
1 2 3 4 5 6 7 8 9 0 LB 00 99 98 97 96

Table of Contents

George Westinghouse was one of America's greatest inventors. By the end of his life, he held 361 patents.

CHAPTER ONE

Growing Up Curious... and Stubborn

George Westinghouse was a difficult child, stubborn and temperamental, yet at the age of 14, he began working on an invention that would earn him his first patent. He was a poor student, considered by many of his teachers to be lazy and inattentive, yet as an adult, he crossed swords with the legendary Thomas Edison—and won. He was a loner with a reputation for being headstrong, yet he grew up to be an enlightened employer who built a model factory town, with affordable housing, schools, and medical facilities for his workers and their families. He was a college dropout, enrolled for less than three months and cutting more classes than he attended, yet by the end of his life, he held 361 patents for inventions that would change the face of America.

George Westinghouse had a genius for invention. The devices he created or sponsored made safe, high-speed train travel a reality, brought electricity and natural gas into American homes and businesses, harnessed the awesome power of Niagara Falls, and illuminated the World's Columbian Exposition of 1893 in Chicago, Illinois, a triumphant celebration of industry and technology.

How did such a headstrong child grow up to be a man who saw—and pursued—possibilities everywhere he looked? The answers to this question can be found by tracing the life and exploring the unique mind of George Westinghouse.

A Small-Town Childhood

George Westinghouse, Jr., was born on October 6, 1846, in Central Bridge, New York, a small village in the Schoharie Valley, 36 miles west of Albany. He was the seventh of ten children born to George and Emmeline Vedder Westinghouse, and he was the second-youngest of the eight who survived infancy. His father's ancestors had come to colonial America from Germany, his mother's from the Netherlands and England. Both families settled in what is now Vermont.

Soon after their marriage, George and Emmeline moved to Ohio farm country, but they did not stay for long. They went back east and settled in New York State. In addition to being a farmer, George, Sr., was a self-taught carpenter and mechanic. He started a small machine-repair shop and in time began manufacturing agricultural machinery. He had at least seven patents to his name for machines used in the

Emmeline Vedder Westinghouse had ten children; George, Jr., was the seventh.

planting and harvesting of crops. Perhaps because he himself did not have a formal education, George, Sr., hoped that his sons would study hard and be successful. During his lifetime, he was to be disappointed in this hope. But it is clear today that one of his sons fulfilled that dream far beyond anything George, Sr., could have imagined.

George Westinghouse, Jr., left no memoirs, unlike many other famous men, and was neither a letter writer nor a journal keeper. What we know about his life comes largely from the people who knew him as an adult. By then, Westinghouse was highly respected as an inventor, industrialist, employer, and family man.

According to some people, however, George was a difficult child. He was prone to temper tantrums and had very few friends. Other people claimed George was a bully, often lashing out in frustration when he was taunted by others. There seems little doubt that school was particularly troublesome for him. He was a poor student, except in math and drawing. He disliked routine study, but left to himself, he showed great curiosity about everything, especially about how things worked. He often played hooky from school, preferring to spend time in his father's machine shop. There he tinkered with scrap materials and was treated as the shop "mascot" by his father's employees.

People with modern attitudes about education and discipline might argue that the type of schooling that George was offered was not compatible with his type of intelligence. In his era, though, he was regarded as a "problem child," and he caused his parents much worry.

When George was ten years old, the family moved to Schenectady, New York, a small city on the banks of the Erie Canal. By then, his younger brother Herman had been born, and the Westinghouse children numbered five boys and three girls. His father's machine-shop business, now called George Westinghouse & Company, had grown, and the family was becoming prosperous.

In 1859, the summer of his thirteenth year, George was permitted to work at his father's company. He was paid 50 cents a day. It was there, in a small workshop built for him in a corner of the attic, that George Westinghouse began tinkering with what would become his first patented invention: a rotary engine.

The work that George, Jr., was paid to do was typical apprentice toil: sweeping the floor, holding tools for more experienced workers, oiling and cleaning the machinery. But one day, according to an often-told tale, he had the chance to show his father how clever he could be. All the workers, except George, had been given a holiday, and the shop was closed for the afternoon. Perhaps to teach George a lesson about the value of diligence, his father had assigned him the task of cutting a large pile of metal pipes into equal lengths. The elder Westinghouse had estimated that the job would take much longer than the afternoon to complete—probably the better part of a week. George set his mind to finding a more efficient way to measure and cut the pipes rather than by hand.

In those days, machine shops were equipped with steam-driven lathes. George knew a thing or two about how these machines worked, because he had often taken them apart to clean them. On that afternoon, he rigged up a cutting device by attaching each pipe to a lathe. The lathe spun each pipe against a stationary cutting blade mounted on the tool rest. Before the afternoon was over, he had reduced the pile to a set of pipes cut perfectly to measure!

The Rotary Engine

George Westinghouse was not the first person to conceive of a rotary engine; nor was he the last. One of the simplest rotary engines is a windmill. Wind pushing against the vanes causes the wheel to turn, and that energy is transferred by means of an axle to the mill's grinding wheel. Another example is a waterwheel, which uses the energy of water falling on blades to turn the wheel around.

Young George's engine was powered by steam. The problem that he sought to solve had to do with the energy that most people thought was "lost," or unused, when the back-and-forth motion of a piston in a reciprocating engine was converted to the circular, or rotary, motion of a wheel.

As it turned out, not much energy is lost in that process. But rotary engines still have an appeal because they can be lighter in weight and because they can have fewer moving parts (which vibrate strongly and can wear out or malfunction) than reciprocating engines. Today, rotary engines—which are also called turbines—are used to power jet airplanes, oceangoing ships, and many electrical power-generating stations.

George Westinghouse probably started out by looking at examples of both rotary and reciprocating generators of power. He had learned to read blueprints in his father's shop and was able to use his drawing talents to sketch his designs. The next step was to build a model, a project that he undertook while in the navy. One account has him testing his engine on a toy boat launched into the Potomac River near where his ship was docked.

Wind gives a simple rotary engine, the windmill, its power. When the wind pushes against the vanes of the windmill, the vanes begin to turn. The energy produced by the turning vanes causes an axle to rotate, generating power.

War Breaks Out

George and his father often disagreed. George, Sr., continued to be disappointed by his son's inattentiveness to his schoolwork—and George, Jr., continued to be more interested in tinkering than in studying. George's restless spirit was further stirred up by the beginning of the Civil War, in 1861.

George was only 14 years old, but he was tall and big for his age. He hatched a plan to run away from home and enlist in the Union forces by lying about his age. This plan was cut short when he was found riding on an eastbound train and his father was summoned to bring him home.

By the eve of his seventeenth birthday, however, two of his older brothers, Albert and John, had already enlisted in the armed forces. George's father finally gave in. In 1863, George joined the army as a private in the Sixteenth New York Volunteer Cavalry. He served in northern Virginia, guarding against raiding parties. A year later, bored with the cavalry, he requested a transfer to the navy. He served for the remainder of the war as acting third assistant engineer

George wanted to join the Union Army when he was 14, but his father wouldn't let him do so until he was almost 17.

on the *Muscoota* and the *Stars and Stripes,* two steam-powered battleships. Their job was to blockade Southern ports. He did not see combat, but with a lathe onboard, George used his idle hours to work on a model of his rotary engine.

His brother Albert, thought to have been his parents' favorite, was killed leading a cavalry charge at McLeod's Mills, Louisiana, in December 1864. George was honorably discharged on June 15, 1865, and when he returned home, it was to a family greatly saddened by Albert's death and all the more determined that George should focus on fulfilling his father's hopes.

War on the Home Front

When he was discharged from the navy, George was nearly 19 years old. He had tasted independence while he was away from his family, and, of course, he had gained experience during the war. The question for him, as for so many young men who had served in the war, was what to do next.

His father, hoping that his tempestuous young son had been sobered by his military service, offered to finance his college education at Schenectady's Union College. George would live at home. From his father's point of view, this meant that he could keep an eye on his son. From George's point of view, it meant that he would have access to his father's shop.

George Westinghouse enrolled in the Science Department at Union College in September 1865. Because of the maturity gained from his war experience and his longtime mechanical ability, he was allowed to skip the freshman year. Nonetheless, his feelings about school were not very different

George Westinghouse, Sr.'s, interest in mechanics greatly influenced his son.

What Is a Patent?

When George Westinghouse applied for his first patent, he was exercising a right guaranteed under Article I, Section 8, of the United States Constitution. Although the first law about patents was passed in 1790, the system for applying for and being granted patents was not established until 1836. Its purpose was to reward inventors for their work and to protect their ideas from being stolen by others.

In the United States, the holder of a patent has the right to prevent others from making, using, or selling the invention for a period of 17 years. During that time, the patent holder may transfer or license it to someone else. After that time, the invention enters what is known as the public domain–anyone can make use of it without restriction. If the inventor makes improvements on the original invention and patents those, then the improved device or process will be protected for another 17 years. As we shall see, George Westinghouse continually made improvements on and added refinements to many of his inventions; in this way, he was able to extend the protection of his patents for many years.

In order for something to be patented, it must be new, useful, novel, and not "obvious...to a person of ordinary skill in the art to which [it]...pertains." A patent can be awarded for any "process, machine, manufacture, or composition of matter, or any new and useful improvement" on any of those.

Patent law is not the same in all countries. Therefore, American patents can be, and often are, violated in other parts of the world. The theft of ideas and innovations patented in the United States has been a serious problem in such countries as China, which does not recognize the validity of American patents. The result is that patent holders lose control of how their inventions are used and fail to share in the financial gain derived from use of their work.

Even in George Westinghouse's time, the details of patenting were complicated, and there were often arguments about who actually invented something first. Today the issue is even more complex, as patents have been sought for computer and telecommunications technology and even for techniques in gene manipulation.

from those of his grade-school days. He found most of the courses boring or irrelevant, and he had difficulty paying attention in class. One professor observed that instead of studying, Westinghouse would amuse himself by making sketches of such things as locomotives and stationary engines. In time, Westinghouse was cutting classes again, spending more time in his attic workshop engaged in his own brand of "independent study."

On October 31, 1865, the U.S. Patent Office awarded Westinghouse patent number 50,759 for his rotary steam engine invention. He had just turned 19, and this patent was the first of the 361 he would eventually obtain over the course of his life.

Being awarded a patent must have made it all the more difficult for George Westinghouse to stay in college. He was full of ideas that he wanted to pursue on his own; attending classes probably seemed like a nuisance.

It is likely, therefore, that he was neither surprised nor particularly disappointed when he was asked to meet with the president of the college. Apparently the two came to the same conclusion: College, for Westinghouse, was a waste of time. With his father's reluctant agreement, he withdrew from Union College during the break for the Christmas and New Year's holidays. With that, George Westinghouse's formal education ended and his life as an inventor began.

CHAPTER TWO

Getting on the Right Track

The new year of 1866 saw George Westinghouse at work as a mechanic in his father's company, earning two dollars a day, a reasonable sum for a young man starting out in those days. George stood at the brink of what his parents hoped would be responsible adulthood. At the same time, the country was also entering a new phase.

The half century between the Civil War and World War I marked the high point of the Industrial Revolution in the United States. It was also a remarkable time for inventors. The northeastern United States in particular was a center of activity for people researching new ways to use electricity. Those five decades of progress coincided with the most productive years of George Westinghouse's life.

The transcontinental railroad inspired George Westinghouse to solve safety problems that he knew were imminent.

Rebuilding a Nation

The aftermath of the American Civil War was a time of social and economic upheaval. The institution of slavery, which had supported the farm-based economy of the South, had come to an end. The modern Industrial Age of factories and assembly lines was about to begin. There was an innovative spirit abroad in the land, and inventors were among the heroes of the day. Many of the new devices were crucial to the field of communications: The telephone, telegraph, typewriter, photograph, radio, and continuous-web printing press all served to strengthen the connections between diverse parts of the country.

There was no force more important in bringing the country together and making possible its rapid expansion than the railroads. In 1830, the first steam-powered railroad was put into regular service. Rail systems underwent considerable growth during the Civil War because both sides relied heavily on trains to transport troops and supplies. In the years following the war, the expansion of the railroads continued hand in hand with the country's territorial expansion. Some 9,000 miles of track had been laid by 1850, most of it in the Atlantic Coast region. At the war's end, in 1865, more than 35,000 miles of track traversed the country; by 1916, that number had grown to 254,000 miles.

The first transcontinental railroad line, linking the East Coast and West Coast via the Union Pacific and Central Pacific Railroads, was opened in 1869. Over the course of the next quarter century, four more transcontinental lines would be built in the United States. But as rail lines began to crisscross the country, the expansion of the rail system brought up an important issue: Unless railroad technology improved, the increased rail traffic would cause insurmountable safety problems. More powerful locomotives, a standard track gauge, or width, as well as better couplers (devices used to join together railroad cars) meant faster and longer trains. But there were also numerous catastrophes, from derailments to collisions, with a high cost in cargo and in human lives. The time was ripe for the mind—and the vision—of George Westinghouse.

A Happy Accident

A number of the tales told about George Westinghouse's life are set on trains. It was on a train, it is said, that he first met the woman who was to become his wife. Another rail journey planted in his mind the idea of an improved train braking system.

Railway accidents helped serve as the force driving Westinghouse's inventive spirit. One story has him on a train in 1866, heading home from Albany, where he had done some business for his father's firm. Westinghouse's train was halted by the derailment of one just ahead of his. This kind of accident was fairly common in those days. Aside from causing extensive delays, it often resulted in injury to passengers and railway workers as well as damage to the cars and the freight they carried.

Westinghouse got off the train to watch as workers labored to inch the heavy cars back onto the track. It took a crew of men wielding crowbars more than two hours to do the job. It occurred to Westinghouse that there was a simpler and faster way to do it. He had conceived the idea of a car replacer—an ingeniously simple device that could be carried on board all trains in case of such an accident.

He quickly drew some sketches and then worked out a model. The car replacer consisted of a short section of rail that could be clamped to the track and then run off at an angle to the derailed car. The locomotive could be steered onto the attached rail, be coupled to the derailed car, and then be put in reverse to pull the car back onto the track. Locomotive power would thus replace manpower. The car replacer became Westinghouse's second patent, which he obtained in February 1867, a little more than a year after he had left college.

His First Company

To finance the car replacer, Westinghouse formed a partnership with two Schenectady businessmen, each of whom put up $5,000. They called the company Rawls, Wall, & Westinghouse. The arrangement combined their money and Westinghouse's toil. The three partners would share profits from the sale of Westinghouse's ideas. Westinghouse would act as salesman. He was only 20 years old when he formed this first company. By the end of his life, Westinghouse would found more than 60 of them.

He quickly added a second device for more efficient railroad transportation, called a reversible frog. A frog is a segment of intersecting rail that allows one track to cross another. Westinghouse's frog, for which he was granted two patents in 1868 and 1869, was innovative in two ways. The first was that it was reversible: When one side wore out, as often occurred, the frog could be flipped over, revealing a

Casting the Industrial Revolution

In choosing cast steel for his reversible frog, George Westinghouse was able to dip into the deep well of invention that existed at the time. In 1855, the British inventor Henry Bessemer had perfected a process for manufacturing low-cost, high-quality steel. This process involved blasting molten iron with air hot enough to oxidize, or burn away, impurities, yielding a stronger metal with a higher melting point. The American headquarters of the Bessemer steelworks was in Troy, New York, only about 15 miles from Schenectady, where George Westinghouse lived.

As was often the case during this period of creativity, another man had had a similar idea. William Kelly, an American, thought up a comparable process and, after battling briefly with Bessemer over patent rights, joined forces with him. The development of steel and the steel industry is one of the most significant chapters in the Industrial Revolution. Steel became the material that built the machines, and the cities, of industrial America and the world.

completely unused surface. The second was that it was made not of cast iron, a brittle alloy that had replaced wooden track in the 1820s, but of cast steel. The combination of the reversible feature and the use of more durable material meant that this frog lasted approximately ten times longer than the ones then in use.

When George Westinghouse became a partner and the salesman for Rawls, Wall, & Westinghouse, he began a new and exciting phase of his life. Although he still lived at home and technically still worked for his father, most of his time was devoted to designing his own products, seeing to their manufacture, and trying to sell them. Traveling to sell his inventions, Westinghouse became considerably more independent than ever before.

His first sale was to the Chicago, Burlington & Quincy Railroad, one of the many independent railway companies that existed at the time. Now that railroads in the United States have been consolidated, selling parts and rolling stock—the wheeled vehicles owned and used by a railroad—is not a very complicated matter. But in George Westinghouse's day, it meant approaching the managers of each railroad and persuading them to give his device a try. But Westinghouse was a good salesman, and he was successful in his endeavor. Before long, a second steel mill, this one in Pompton, New Jersey, was engaged to manufacture the car replacer and the reversible frog.

A Whirlwind Courtship, a Partnership for Life

Fittingly, it was on a train journey, this time returning home to Schenectady from nearby Troy, that Westinghouse met a young woman named Marguerite Erskine Walker. A resident of Roxbury, New York, she was on her way to Kingston after visiting some relatives in Brooklyn. They struck up a conversation, and soon George was smitten. He later said of himself that he had always known what he wanted. When he said this, he was referring to his professional life. It seems, however, that he knew what he wanted in his personal life as well. The two were married on August 8, 1867, making their first home with George's parents. By all accounts, the marriage, which lasted until George's death in 1914, was a strong and happy one.

George and Marguerite Westinghouse enjoyed a long and happy life together. Here, they are pictured at their son's wedding in England in 1909.

Much later, when he was an extremely wealthy man, Westinghouse constructed a summer estate in Lenox, Massachusetts, and named it Erskine Park, in recognition of his wife's family. George and Marguerite had one child, George Westinghouse III, born in 1883. Marguerite died a mere three months after her husband, in June 1914, and is buried next to him in Arlington National Cemetery, in Washington, D.C.

Another Train, Another Idea

Although we have to rely on the words of others for many of the facts about George Westinghouse's life, he has left an account of the event that started him thinking about a better way to stop a train:

> *My first idea of braking apparatus to be applied to all of the cars of a train came to me in this way; a train upon which I was a passenger between Schenectady and Troy in 1866 was delayed a couple of hours due to a collision between two freight trains. The loss of time and the inconvenience arising from it suggested that if the engineers of those trains had had some means of applying brakes to all of the wheels of their trains, the accident in question might have been avoided and the time of my fellow-passengers and myself might have been saved.*
>
> *The first idea which came into my mind, which I afterwards found had been in the minds of many others, was to connect the brake levers of each car to its draft-gear so that an application of the brakes to the locomotive, which would cause the cars to close up toward the engine, would thereby apply a*

braking force through the couplers and levers to the wheels of each car. Although the crudeness of this idea became apparent upon an attempt to devise an apparatus to carry the scheme into effect, nevertheless the idea of applying power brakes to a train was firmly planted in my mind.

This anecdote provides a vivid picture of how the wheels of invention would begin to turn in Westinghouse's head. A look at the puzzle he was trying to solve—a new way of stopping a train, a problem desperately in need of a solution—shows how this event led to Westinghouse's first great enterprise.

In the days when George Westinghouse was traveling from town to town selling his car replacer and reversible frog, trains consisted of a steam locomotive, its tender (an attached vehicle for carrying fuel and water), and no more than five or six cars. Speeds of ten miles an hour were usually the maximum allowed, because at greater speeds, a train would take far too long to stop. As it was, scheduled stops required at least one mile's notice; emergency stops often occurred too late. In both instances, stopping was a jolting experience.

The engineer would signal that a stop was needed by sounding a whistle while simultaneously shutting down the throttle to the engine. The "down brakes" whistle told the crew of five or six brakemen, one stationed between each two cars, that it was time to begin their strenuous labor. As the coasting train approached its intended stop, each brakeman turned a horizontal brake wheel, which tightened a heavy chain, forcing the brake shoes against the wheels of the car. Once one brake wheel was tightened, the brakeman rushed to turn another. Turning the wheel on the moving train took so much strength that the hand-turned brake was nicknamed the "Armstrong."

As the friction of the brake shoes caused the wheels of the car to stop turning, that car would come to a halt. If the car in front of or behind it did not slow and stop at the same rate—and that was frequently the case—the cars would knock into each other, jolting the passengers and upsetting crates and cases in the baggage cars. On freight trains, the brake wheels were on the top of each car. This was very hazardous for the brakemen, many of whom were injured and even killed as they ran across the tops of the cars from brake to brake.

At the very least, trains either overshot or stopped short of the station, which would require the engineer to throw the locomotive into reverse or to open up the throttle again so that the train could limp into the station. Collisions were extremely common and often deadly. Clearly, if America expected to steam into the future, a more efficient braking system had to be devised.

Westinghouse knew that the answer was to apply all the brakes at the same time, and the engineer seemed to be the one to do it. But how?

An Idea Whose Time Had Come

As Westinghouse recalled, he was not the only person to see the problem with the current brake system or to envision a solution. His first idea was to equip the engine cab with a huge wheel, called a windlass, that would tighten a chain that ran the length of the train and was attached to the braking mechanism of each car. In the course of his travels for

Rawls, Wall, & Westinghouse, George found himself at the yards of the Chicago, Burlington & Quincy Railroad in Chicago. There he saw a braking device that employed such a design and met its inventor, a man named Ambler. Ambler's system used the locomotive's driving wheel to turn the windlass.

Upon seeing the actual mechanism, Westinghouse realized that a train longer than the typical five or six cars would require a chain so heavy and a windlass so huge that there would be room in the cab for little else—not even for the engineer. Westinghouse came up with the idea of using the steam from the locomotive to drive a piston through a cylinder beneath the locomotive, "...to be so connected to the chain that it could be drawn tight...with a force that could be more accurately controlled than was possible with the windlass arrangement."

As it turned out, however, the piston-driven chain brake was also limited to four or five cars. As with Ambler's contraption, a longer train would call for a chain so long, and therefore so heavy, that a steam cylinder almost as large as the locomotive itself would be required. Westinghouse knew that future trains would be made up of a dozen cars or more, so he had to figure out a way to stop a longer train.

What followed is a true example of trial and error, with a dose of happy coincidence. In a pattern that would repeat itself in the creation of most of Westinghouse's work, he pondered an idea, made drawings, experimented with models, discovered flaws, then went back to the drawing board. Rather than finding this process discouraging, he seems to have enjoyed not only the challenge but also the opportunity to bring together ideas from his own growing storehouse and those of other inventors and engineers.

The Straight-Air Brake

Westinghouse's first air brake, in 1869, is known as the straight-air brake. This device consisted of an air pump driven by a steam engine powered by the same boiler that supplied steam to the locomotive; a holding tank, or reservoir, also located in the locomotive, to hold air compressed by the pump; a pipe leading from the reservoir to a valve controlled by the engineer; brake cylinders under each car; and a length of pipe running from the control valve under all cars of the train, with connections to each brake cylinder branching out from the pipe.

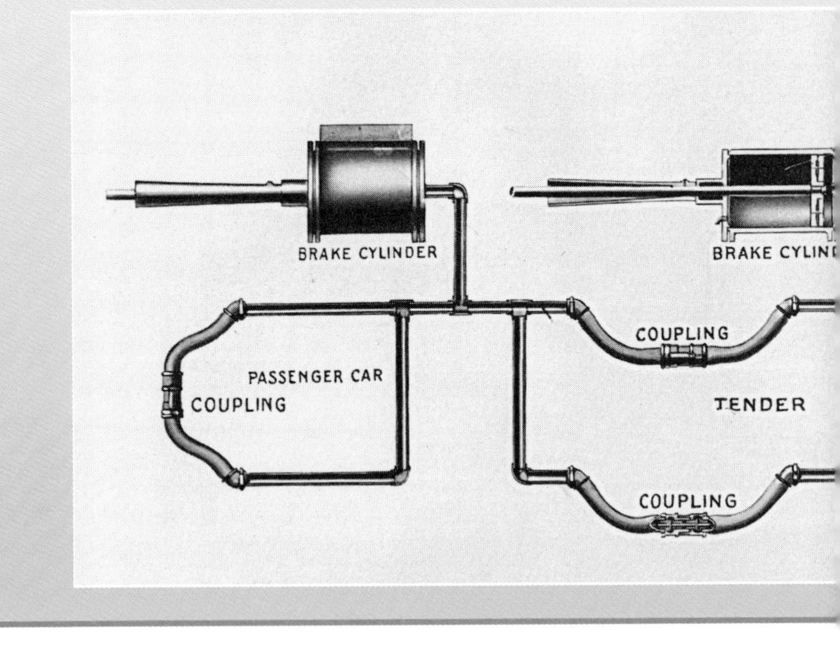

This interest in the ideas and achievements of others also served him well in his later endeavors. Time after time, when Westinghouse heard or read of an inventor developing an idea that he thought had promise, he would adapt it to a project of his own. If the inventor held a patent on the

When the engineer wanted to stop the train, he opened the valve, which released compressed air from the reservoir and sent it rushing through the pipe to the end of the train. Along the way, the pressure forced open a valve leading into each cylinder and pushed the piston housed inside. That, in turn, pushed the brake shoe against the wheel. To release the brake, the engineer closed the reservoir valve and opened a different valve, which released the air in the pipe into the atmosphere. As the pressure dropped, the pistons moved back in the cylinders and the brake shoes moved out of contact with the wheels. The entire procedure for stopping the train was thereby controlled by a single person–the engineer.

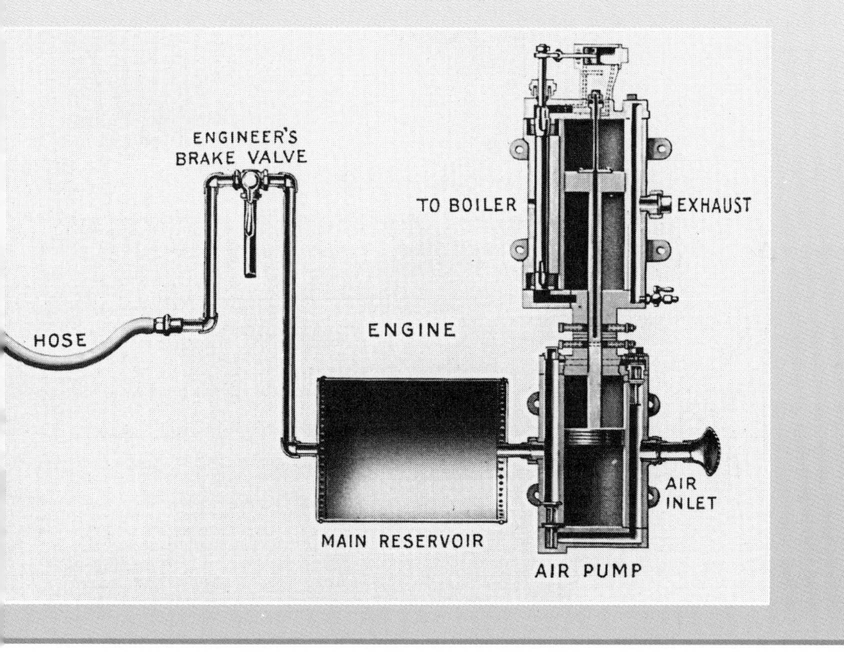

idea or the device, he would pay in order to be able to use it. In a manner that was always fair and honest, and often outstandingly generous, he made the most of the inventive spirit that was so prevalent in America, and even throughout Europe, at the time.

By his own account, Westinghouse's next step in his quest to solve the braking problem was to run a pipe from the locomotive along the full length of the train. It would be attached to the underside of each car. There would be a flexible connection between cars to prevent the pipe from snapping as a result of the movement of the train. Steam would be carried through the pipe and would activate a piston-and-cylinder arrangement fitted to each car. However, Westinghouse discarded the idea when it became clear that even in warm weather, the steam would condense long before it reached the end of the train. In cold weather, the condensed steam would likely freeze.

It would seem that, steam being the most powerful moving force widely available at the time, Westinghouse had run up against a brick wall. Fortunately, there was a solution, and it came to his attention only by chance.

One day, while grappling with the problem in his father's factory, Westinghouse was interrupted by two young women who were selling subscriptions to a monthly magazine called *The Living Age*. George agreed to subscribe, and, in what he remembered as the first issue, he found an article that held the answer to his problem.

The article, about a tunnel being built through Mont Cenis, in the Swiss Alps, described steam-powered machinery as being clearly impractical for boring deep into the rock. Steam, which is made by heating water, required a source of heat (in those days, it was burning coal or wood), which in turn required oxygen. Oxygen was in short supply inside the tunnel, and the workers needed all that was available and perhaps even more just to breathe. Generating the steam outside the tunnel and piping it in might have worked, but only up to a point. The tunnel had reached a depth of 3,000 feet, much too far for steam pressure to travel. The solution was to use compressed air, which served the dual purpose of driving the drilling machinery and providing additional air for the workers.

Westinghouse instantly understood that compressed air was a force he could apply to his own project. He now concentrated on working out every detail of the plan. He designed an air-compressor that would be operated by steam from the locomotive boiler. The engineer could easily admit compressed air into the braking system to stop the train. The engineer could also release air from the system to release the brakes. Westinghouse even designed the couplings for the air pipes located between train cars. Valves automatically opened when the pipes were joined, and they automatically closed when the pipes were apart. George Westinghouse submitted paperwork for a patent in July 1868, and it was granted on April 13, 1869. It was the first of 103 patents related to air brakes that he would receive over the course of the next 38 years.

At the same time that Westinghouse was working out the earliest details of his braking system, his business arrangement with his partners Rawls and Wall was coming apart. Westinghouse may have been excited by his newest idea, but his partners were disappointed by the small profits they were making. For them, the partnership was a business proposition—and business was not booming.

In 1868, Rawls and Wall told Westinghouse that they would be running the business without his involvement. Westinghouse was stunned and infuriated by their decision to push him out of the business.

The arrangement that Westinghouse had originally made gave the rights to his patents to the company that the three men had formed, not to any single individual. As Westinghouse saw it, when the partnership was dissolved, the patent rights should be returned to him. As his partners saw it, they still had the rights to his two devices even if he was no longer a partner. It was a sticky situation, but one thing became clear to Westinghouse: He would not share any of his new ideas, especially not that of the air brake, with those two men.

Westinghouse must have felt betrayed by his former partners, although we have only the words of others to attest to that. It was likely that he emerged much wiser from the experience. As a partner in his first business, he had certainly broadened his horizons. He had traveled to many cities, met many people in the railroad and manufacturing industries, and acquired a greater understanding of how business worked.

Westinghouse had been investigating moving the manufacture of his car replacer and reversible frog to a steel mill in Pittsburgh, Pennsylvania, which, he hoped, could produce the devices less expensively than could the mills in Troy and Pompton. He decided to travel to Pittsburgh to discuss his business in person.

It was there that he met Ralph Baggaley, a man who would become both a close friend and a trusted business associate. And it was that trip that started the chain of events that have linked the names of Westinghouse and Pittsburgh ever since.

CHAPTER THREE

Making Connections to Build an Empire

When George Westinghouse arrived in Pittsburgh, late in the year 1868, he headed for the offices of Anderson and Cook, the steel mill that he hoped would take over the manufacture of his rail devices. Uncertain of his way in the new city, he asked directions from a young man he met on the street. The two struck up a conversation, during which Westinghouse described his business in Pittsburgh. His new companion, Ralph Baggaley, mentioned that he worked for a foundry, a metal casting factory. In this chance meeting, Westinghouse had found a friend with whom he had a lot in common.

When he was in his thirties, George Westinghouse's mature appearance may have been helpful to him in dealing with older, more experienced railroad owners.

Westinghouse's meeting with the managers of Anderson and Cook was equally rewarding. They agreed to manufacture his car replacer and reversible frog at their own expense, if Westinghouse would act as salesman. Although he was taking a big risk by defying his ex-partners, Westinghouse made a wise career move: Not only did this new arrangement give him a modest income while he continued working on his own projects, but it brought him into contact with railroad people and helped familiarize him with what they needed. It also gave him a chance to try out his ideas on potential customers and to get their suggestions for improvements. Today, this business strategy is called networking and marketing research.

Another step still taken today in the marketing of a product is the creation of a prototype, a working model that can be demonstrated. Making such a model costs money, which Westinghouse did not have. His father, convinced that his son was reaching beyond himself in an irresponsible way, was unwilling to help. George, Jr., had married with the hope of being able to support his wife on earnings from his car replacer, yet the couple was still living in his parents' home. That business had fallen apart and now he was proposing an even greater financial risk. The elder Westinghouse refused to have anything to do with it. Fortunately, for Westinghouse and for history, Ralph Baggaley was interested enough in his new friend's ideas that he agreed to put up the money needed to make a full-size model of the straight-air brake. They rigged it up, as though on a train, on the floor of a Pittsburgh machine shop.

Through his contacts in the railroad business, Westinghouse invited officials of the Pennsylvania and Panhandle Railroads to watch the demonstration. Among those who came was Alexander Cassatt, who would become the president of the Pennsylvania Railroad and the driving force behind the construction of New York City's Pennsylvania Station. Another was W. W. Card, who was superintendent of the smaller Panhandle Railroad.

Although both men were impressed with the demonstration, persuading them to finance a trial run on an actual train was another matter. Cassatt said no, but Card agreed to ask his superiors at Panhandle if they would sponsor the project. In the end, officials of the Panhandle Railroad agreed to lend Westinghouse one of their trains. However, he would have to pay for the installation and removal of his prototype device. The offer was too good to turn down, and with Baggaley's moral and financial support, Westinghouse set to work.

The Trial Run

One morning in April 1869, the *Steubenville Accommodation,* which consisted of a locomotive, a tender, and three passenger cars, steamed out of Pittsburgh's Union Station, bound for Steubenville, Ohio. Attached to the underside of the train was Westinghouse's prototype braking system. The passengers included the nervous inventor himself and officials of the Panhandle Railroad, among them W. W. Card.

Although Westinghouse and the engineer, Dan Tate, had agreed that a number of stops would be made at different speeds, little did they suspect that it would be an emergency stop that would prove the value of the air brake.

Grant's Hill tunnel carried trains from Union Station to what was then the far side of the city. The train steamed out

Pneumatics: The Power of Compressed Air

Although we cannot see it, air exerts pressure on us even under normal conditions. The way we most commonly experience this is when we feel the wind blowing. It can be strong enough to fill a sail and push a boat across a stretch of water. A sneeze is another way to feel the force of air under pressure.

Normal air pressure at sea level is 14.7 pounds per square inch (psi) or one kilogram per square centimeter, a unit called one atmosphere. George Westinghouse's air brake compressed air to a level of 70 psi, nearly five atmospheres. That pressure was achieved by forcing steam into a closed chamber called a reservoir. The pressure was maintained in a closed system as it traveled through the narrow pipe under the train and pushed the pistons that moved the brake shoes. The pressure dropped when the system was opened, allowing the steam to expand into the atmosphere.

The use of air under pressure to drive a device is called pneumatics. A primitive pneumatic device is a bellows. A hand pump used to inflate a bicycle tire is another pneumatic device.

Pneumatic devices were common in the days before electricity was harnessed. They are useful even today in places such as underground mines, where it is too hazardous to use electricity because of the danger of fire or explosions.

of the tunnel at a speed of 30 miles per hour. To his horror, Tate saw a horse and cart crossing the tracks just a few yards ahead. He immediately threw the switch to set the brakes and, to the amazement of all, the train came to a full stop within mere feet of the startled horse and driver.

As Westinghouse recalled, the engineer's immediate application of the air brakes prevented what could have been a very serious accident, thus instantaneously proving the great value of this invention. As a result, Westinghouse's air brake started on its road to success.

The success of the trial run was enough to encourage George to go full steam ahead with his braking system. This time, he was able to line up financial backers who knew railroads and, in several cases, ran them. In September 1869, the Westinghouse Air Brake Company was founded. Its board of directors included Ralph Baggaley as well as W. W. Card, of the Panhandle Railroad, and Robert Pitcairn, Edward H.

This was the first train equipped by George Westinghouse with compressed-air power brakes for regular road service.

Williams, and Alexander Cassatt, of the Pennsylvania Railroad. Its president was George Westinghouse, just a month shy of age 23.

The new company's first task was to try out the brake system on longer trains and, in doing so, to win over the other railroads. That September, a six-car Pennsylvania Railroad train equipped with Westinghouse brakes made a run from Pittsburgh to Altoona, Pennsylvania, through the steep and curving passes of the Allegheny Mountains. In October, the system was tested on a ten-car Pennsylvania Railroad train bound for Philadelphia. Later on, trains equipped with the straight-air brake traveled as far as Chicago and Indianapolis, effectively demonstrating to railroad managers and the public alike how sure and safe George Westinghouse's new system was.

Although many railroads resisted Westinghouse's innovation at first, he eventually got orders from the Michigan Central and Chicago & Northwestern Railroads, then from the Union Pacific, Old Colony, and Boston & Providence lines. Passenger trains were now typically 12 cars long and weighed in excess of 250 tons, but a train traveling 30 miles an hour could come to a full stop in just 500 feet if it was equipped with a Westinghouse air brake. Clearly, things had come a long way since it had taken the muscle power of six men the distance of a mile to stop a train going only ten miles per hour.

One of the toughest nuts to crack, but also one of the most important, was the New York Central Railroad, owned by the formidable Cornelius Vanderbilt. But in 1871, after a New York Central train collided with a freight train and plunged off a bridge over Wappinger's Creek, killing 30 people and injuring scores of others, Vanderbilt placed an

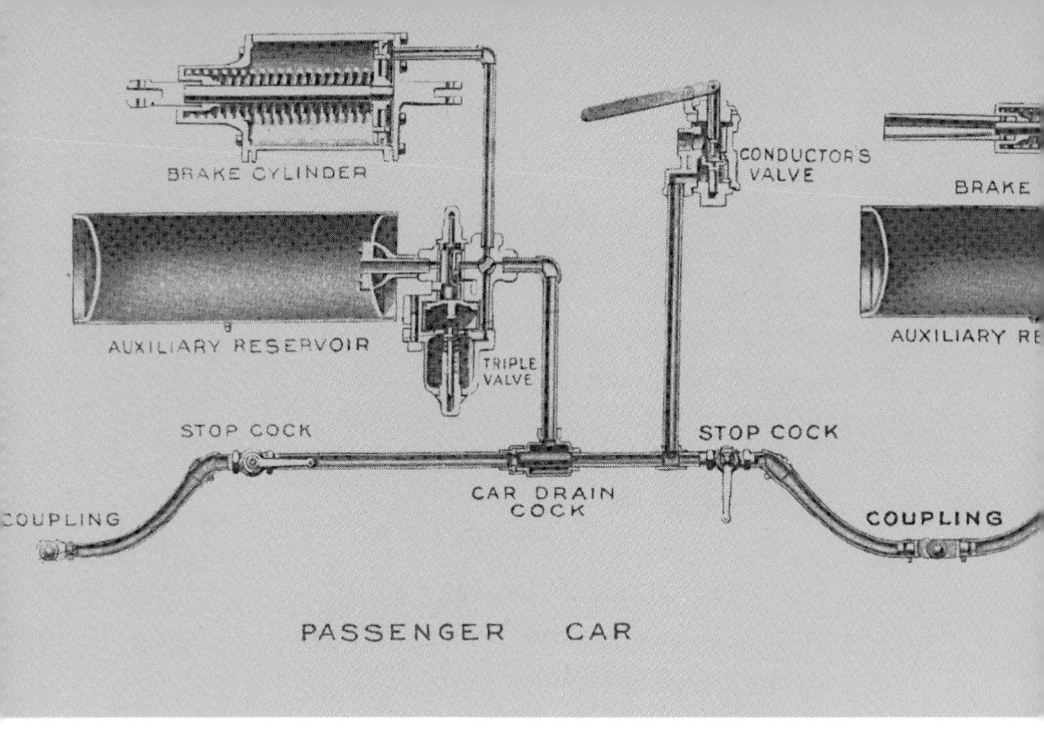

The Westinghouse plain automatic air brake system of 1872 was a major milestone in rail technology. In this system, brakes would automatically be applied if train cars became separated.

order for Westinghouse brakes for all New York Central passenger trains.

By 1874, a mere five years after that first trial run, 2,281 locomotives and 7,254 railroad cars were equipped with the straight-air brake, including 148 locomotives and 724 cars in countries outside the United States. By 1876, nearly 38 percent of all railroad cars and locomotives in the United States boasted the Westinghouse brake.

As effective as the straight-air brake was, however, it was far from perfect. Early on, Westinghouse was well aware of its weaknesses. He observed that it took a considerable amount of time to apply the brakes with full force. It also took a long time to release them. What is more, if a train broke in two—a frequent occurrence in those days—the engineer would not be able to control the rear section of the train. If this happened while going up a hill, the rear

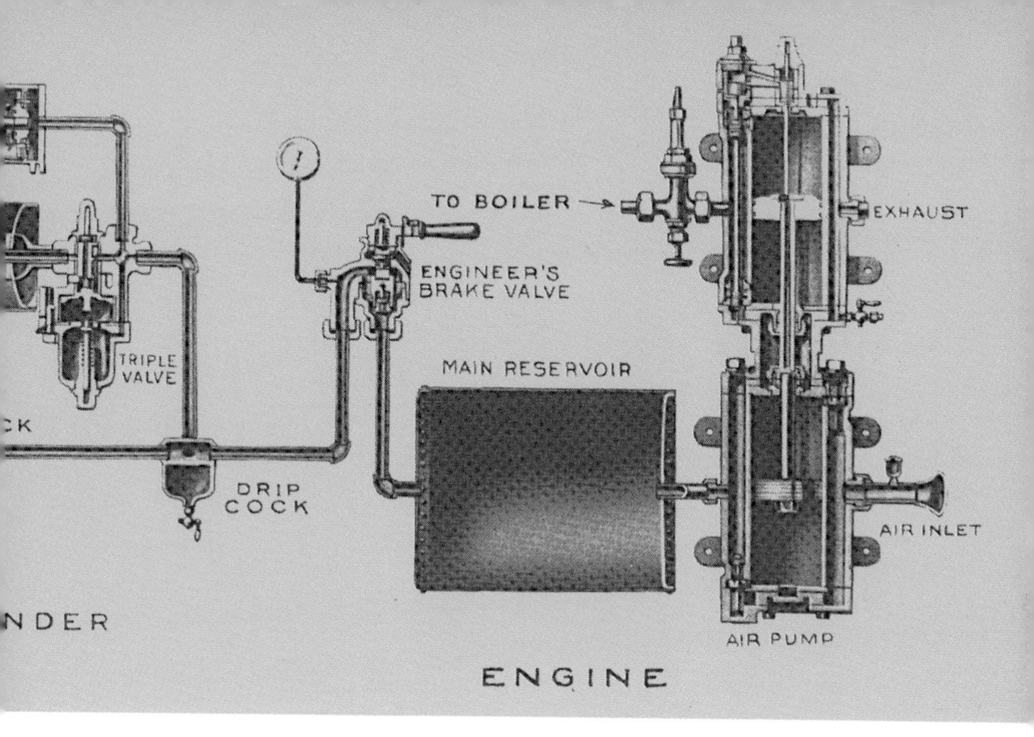

detached section of the train might run away—a possible disaster.

It was in the way that he addressed this problem that Westinghouse showed his true genius: He arrived at the answer by turning the problem on its head. The failure to stop a moving train can spell disaster; but if a stopped train will not move, it is simply an inconvenience. Why not have trains stop when there is no pressure and move only when there is pressure? That way, an accidental loss of pressure will not have disastrous results.

That is the principle behind the automatic air brake. While an increase of air pressure in the train pipe applies the brakes in the straight-air braking system, a *decrease* of pressure applies the brakes in the automatic system. Therefore, if a train breaks apart, the brakes automatically go on and the detached cars come to a halt.

Between 1872 and 1876, Westinghouse worked on improving the air brake, taking out 11 patents on different features of the automatic system. Moreover, each of the improvements could be added to the standard straight-air brake so that trains equipped with the early version could be upgraded, thus avoiding total replacement of the system. It was a clever marketing move as well.

From Tinkerer to Tycoon

By now, the impetuous young man who had thought of a better way to keep trains on track was a considerably more mature man. Now in his thirties and a name to be reckoned with, George Westinghouse was a company president, an associate of American railroad magnates, and an important figure in Europe as well. By the mid-1870s, he had opened branches of his company in England, France, and Russia. He frequently traveled to Europe to oversee operations, find new customers, and learn what was new in the railroad world abroad.

In Europe, as in the United States, the transportation revolution that Westinghouse had helped to set in motion had gathered steam. Controlling the increased rail traffic was the next major challenge. And, as usual, George Westinghouse was at the forefront, his singular curiosity and tenacity driving him onward.

Railroad-traffic control in the United States was still a primitive affair in 1880, a collection of signals and switches directly controlled by workers rather than automatically. Signals do more than just indicate that a train can proceed along a track. They also give information on reducing or

By the time he was in his thirties, George Westinghouse was the head of a major company. He is shown here with his wife, Marguerite.

increasing speed. Because a wide variety of trains use the same tracks, at different speeds and for different purposes, such information is critical for safety. What is more, the information is essential if railroad companies are to use trains and tracks efficiently.

In 1880, for example, a railroad worker would receive a telegraphed message to clear the track. The worker would activate a signal, which in turn would alert others to move switches by hand. The switches ensured that the train would move from one track to another. But this system was filled with potential for error. A worker might fall asleep and neglect to activate a signal, for instance. Any number of actions—or lack of action—could cause an accident.

George Westinghouse was not the first to recognize that improvements were needed. The English had developed a more sophisticated system known as block signaling. Through his international connections, Westinghouse was able to study the English system and come up with ways to adapt it and improve it for use at home.

The English system relied on blocking, or reserving a length of track for each train. When signaled, workers would open the switches to admit the train, then close them so that no other trains could enter the block of track until that train had passed through it. A refinement of the block system used interlocking switches and signals: Instead of being opened and closed by hand, the switch was controlled by the same mechanism that controlled the signal. That prevented conflicting signals—and collisions.

By 1890, all British passenger rails were equipped with interlocking switches and signals. But in 1880, when George Westinghouse first started thinking about how to improve the system, nothing of the kind existed in the United States.

The railroad companies did not even recognize the need for change. Westinghouse, who always saw the big picture, was faced with two tasks: As an inventor, he had to come up with an effective system. And as a businessman, he had to convince his potential customers that they needed his product. It took 20 years to accomplish these two goals. Eventually, however, the Westinghouse vision and dogged persistence paid off.

Faced with general skepticism, but considerably wiser in the ways of business than he had been in his early twenties, George Westinghouse was determined not to risk the profits of investors in his now-successful brake company. In 1881, he formed a new enterprise with his own money. He called it the Union Switch and Signal Company. Westinghouse's switch-and-signal system proved to be the perfect partner of his automatic brake. While the development of the automatic brake was a momentous event in the transportation revolution, the brake needed automatic switching and signaling to function to its full potential. Each new innovation naturally complemented the other.

Back to the Drawing Board

Starting with the idea of an interlocking system, Westinghouse turned his attention to making it automatic. He knew that relying only on human strength and attentiveness would limit the usefulness of any device. The power of compressed air, or pneumatics, which worked so well in the air brake, immediately came to mind. However, it was one thing to attach a steam pipe to a train—and another thing entirely to attach it to a track. Aboveground

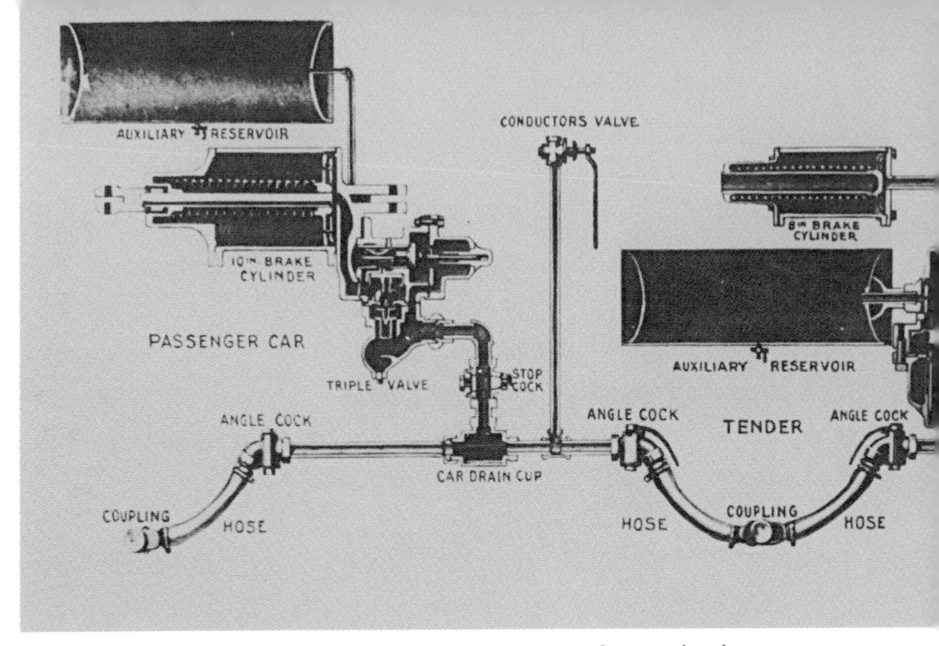

Westinghouse continued to make improvements on his work. This diagram shows his 1887 quick action automatic air brake system.

pipes would be easily damaged and underground piping, if damaged, would have to be dug up for repair.

Westinghouse next thought about combining electricity and pneumatics, using compressed air for the heavy work and electricity to start the function. The track could conduct an electrical current, which would activate the compressed-air switch. As a safety feature, an open switch or damaged section of track would act as a circuit breaker. In that way, the go-ahead signal would not be given, and so a train would not stray onto that section of track. This device involved the same kind of thinking that had led to the improved air brake: A failure in the system would prevent the train from moving, and thereby prevent a disaster.

At the time, however, electrified tracks were considered too dangerous. Westinghouse then considered the possibility of using hydraulic, or water pressure, but water could freeze and disable the system. It took ten years of trial and error, but Westinghouse finally devised a safe way to use electricity—with heavy and durable insulation.

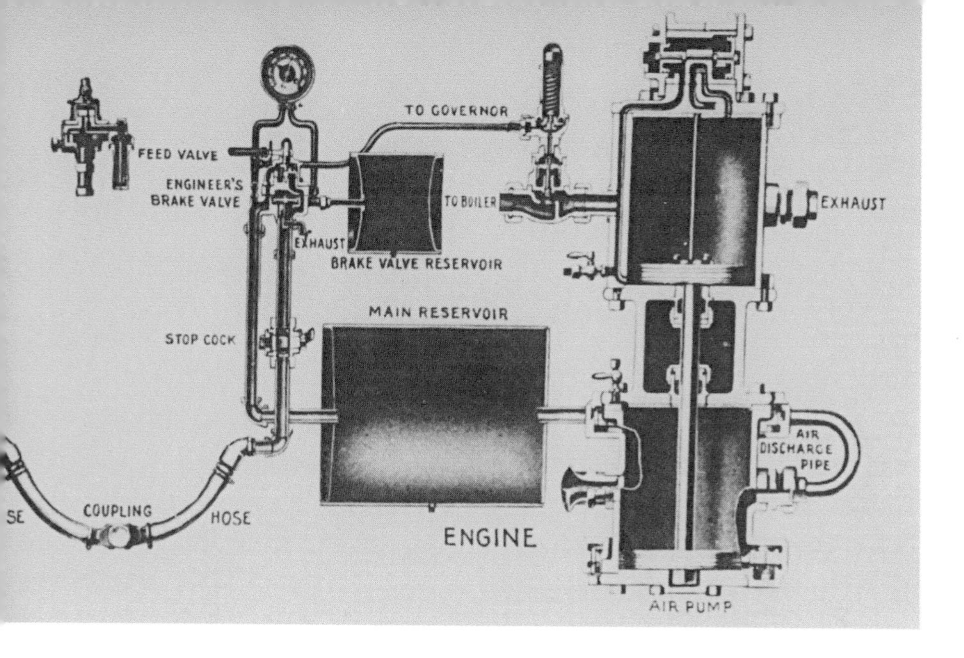

Over the course of the decade, he continued to refine the air brake and to work on other train-related devices. One very important device was the friction draft gear, which saved wear and tear on the couplings between cars. Although it was considerably less complex than his air brake and interlocking signals, many people think it was his greatest contribution to railroading.

To put it simply, when a train comes to a stop, the energy of its forward momentum is absorbed by heavy springs in the connections between the cars as they move together. As the brakes are released, the springs release the energy and the cars move away from each other. Over time, this back-and-forth movement causes the couplings to wear out. Westinghouse's mechanism included metal plates, which created friction as the couplings pushed against the springs. The energy spent on overcoming the friction reduced the energy that was absorbed, and eventually released, by the springs. The idea was simple, but the savings in time, money, and potential disaster have been considerable.

A New Direction

If George Westinghouse's only contributions had been in the field of railroad transportation, his name and legacy would be sufficiently important to go down in the history books. But in 1883, his imagination took him in a new direction, and an entirely different field opened up to him. As it had before, however, his ability to see the big picture, to follow through from an idea to a product, and to build on knowledge and experience gained in earlier work, all served him well.

The new field was energy, and this time the energy source was natural gas. Although he was not the first person to bring natural gas into Pittsburgh, he did refine ways of accessing and delivering it.

Once again, Westinghouse was spurred on by a lucky accident, this time a very dramatic one.

The days of living with his parents were long over, and Westinghouse had bought a mansion befitting a successful tycoon and his wife. It was named Solitude, and it stood in a parklike setting on the outskirts of Pittsburgh. It occurred to Westinghouse that the natural gas abundant in wells under much of the city might also be found on his property. Almost as a lark, he arranged to have a test well dug behind his stables.

One night in February 1884, long past midnight, after he and Marguerite had gone to sleep, they were awakened by a thunderous explosion. The test well had hit a huge pocket of natural gas a bit more than 1,500 feet below the ground.

After a week, and with considerable effort, the well was finally capped. It was fitted with a valve, which allowed a more controlled flow of gas. Westinghouse, who had always

Cooking and Lighting with Gas

When Thomas Edison received a patent for his electric lamp, which is the ancestor of today's lightbulb, it signaled the end of the gaslight era. But it would take more than the power from a glowing glass globe to complete the transformation from the day-to-day use of gas to electricity.

Edison's lamp required electricity, an energy source that was not available to most people living in the United States. In fact, until George Westinghouse entered the picture, American homes that were lit by electricity were owned only by people who were very rich and who could afford to maintain their own electrical generators. Most people still used gas to light the lanterns in their homes. Gas was also frequently used for heating homes and buildings and for cooking meals.

In the late nineteenth century, the most widely used gas was made from coal. It was pumped from the gasworks, where it was manufactured, through underground pipes that led to homes, businesses, and streetlights. Natural gas was also available, in what seemed like limitless quantities.

Natural gas is an odorless, flammable substance trapped within the Earth's crust. It is actually a mixture of gases. The predominant gas is methane. Natural gas is one of the most abundant fossil fuels—substances that are formed by the decay of plants and animals. Natural gas can be found alongside oil and coal deposits throughout the world. Like coal and oil, however, it is an energy source that is non-renewable—once we have used up all the natural gas available, we will not be able to replace it by making more.

Pockets of natural gas are always under enormous pressure, which makes the threat of explosion and fire very real. It is a danger that George Westinghouse experienced firsthand. He virtually eliminated the danger, however, by discovering a way to make natural gas a safe, valuable source of energy for household, commercial, and industrial use.

been somewhat flamboyant, now played the showman. He ignited the gas jet, which burst into a roaring torch rising a hundred feet into the air, visible for miles throughout the entire neighborhood.

After he had had his fun, Westinghouse set his mind to practical matters. The first thing he did was to form yet another company, the Philadelphia Company. Next on his agenda was to develop a way to make the well useful. The name of his first natural-gas patent—"System for Conveying and Utilizing Gas Under Pressure"—says it all.

The task at hand was to control the enormous pressure of the natural gas as it came out of the earth and carry it through a populated area without risking explosion and leakage. Westinghouse achieved his goal by constructing a pipeline that gradually widened and in so doing gradually lowered the pressure of the gas traveling through it. By the time the gas arrived at a home or a factory, the pressure would be low enough to be safe yet high enough to keep a flame burning.

In 1884 and 1885, Westinghouse developed and patented 28 inventions related to natural gas, including well-digging methods, leak detectors, air regulators, and gas meters.

One of the results of Westinghouse's success in making this inexpensive fuel accessible was that it brought industry to Pittsburgh. Because of its access to inexpensive energy, within a very short time, the city would become a major industrial center and the steelmaking capital of the United States, if not the world.

The idea of transforming a hugely powerful force into a manageable one over a distance was one that would stay with Westinghouse. He would turn to it again, this time to transport another, vastly more important source of energy.

CHAPTER FOUR

Becoming a Man of Power

In an age when the flick of a switch and the click of a mouse are familiar routines, it is difficult to imagine a time when electricity was not taken for granted. Back in the 1880s, however, the use of electrical power was still in its infancy. Like today's information superhighway, the new technology was exciting, but people were not yet sure about the best way to use it. For many people in Westinghouse's time, an electrified world seemed to be a potentially dangerous place.

George Westinghouse was convinced that it was a world of limitless possibilities. As he had often done before, he saw a need. Industry was growing rapidly in the United States, and he knew that the country could no longer depend on steam. Developing more powerful and more efficient energy sources was essential. By this time in his life, he had gained the experience and the resources to launch a full-scale effort to turn those possibilities into reality.

The Earliest Spark

The age of electricity began in 1831, when Michael Faraday, in England, and Joseph Henry, in the United States, made an important discovery at almost the same time. Working independently, both men found that an electrical current could be created, or induced, by moving a simple magnet through the center of a wire coil. The next step was to invent a

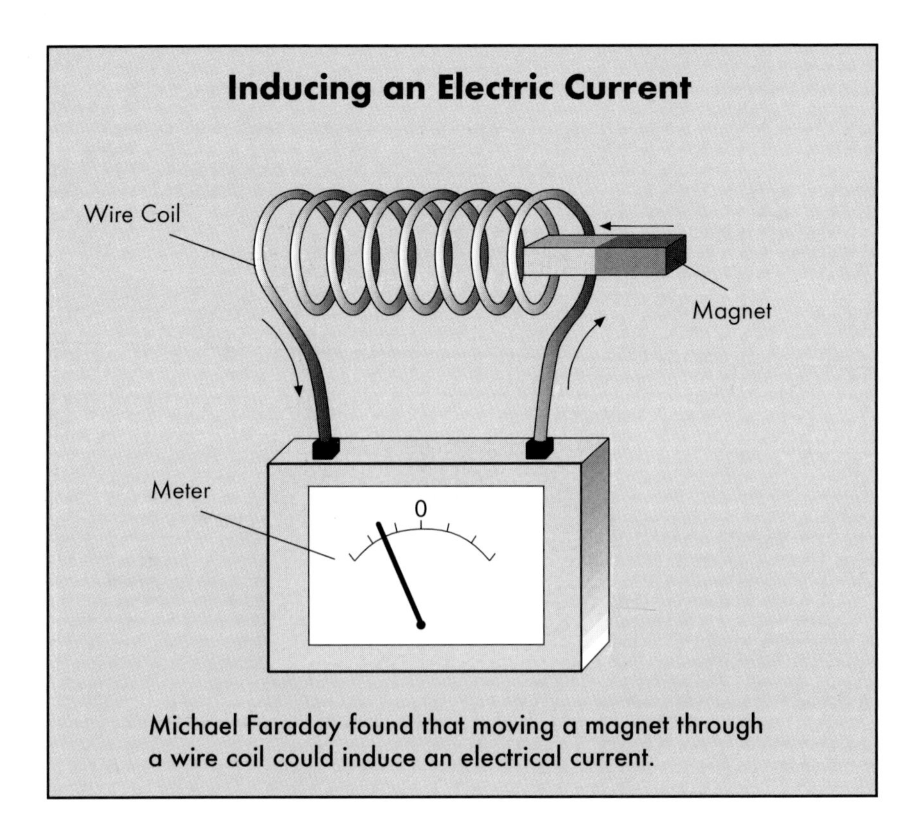

Michael Faraday found that moving a magnet through a wire coil could induce an electrical current.

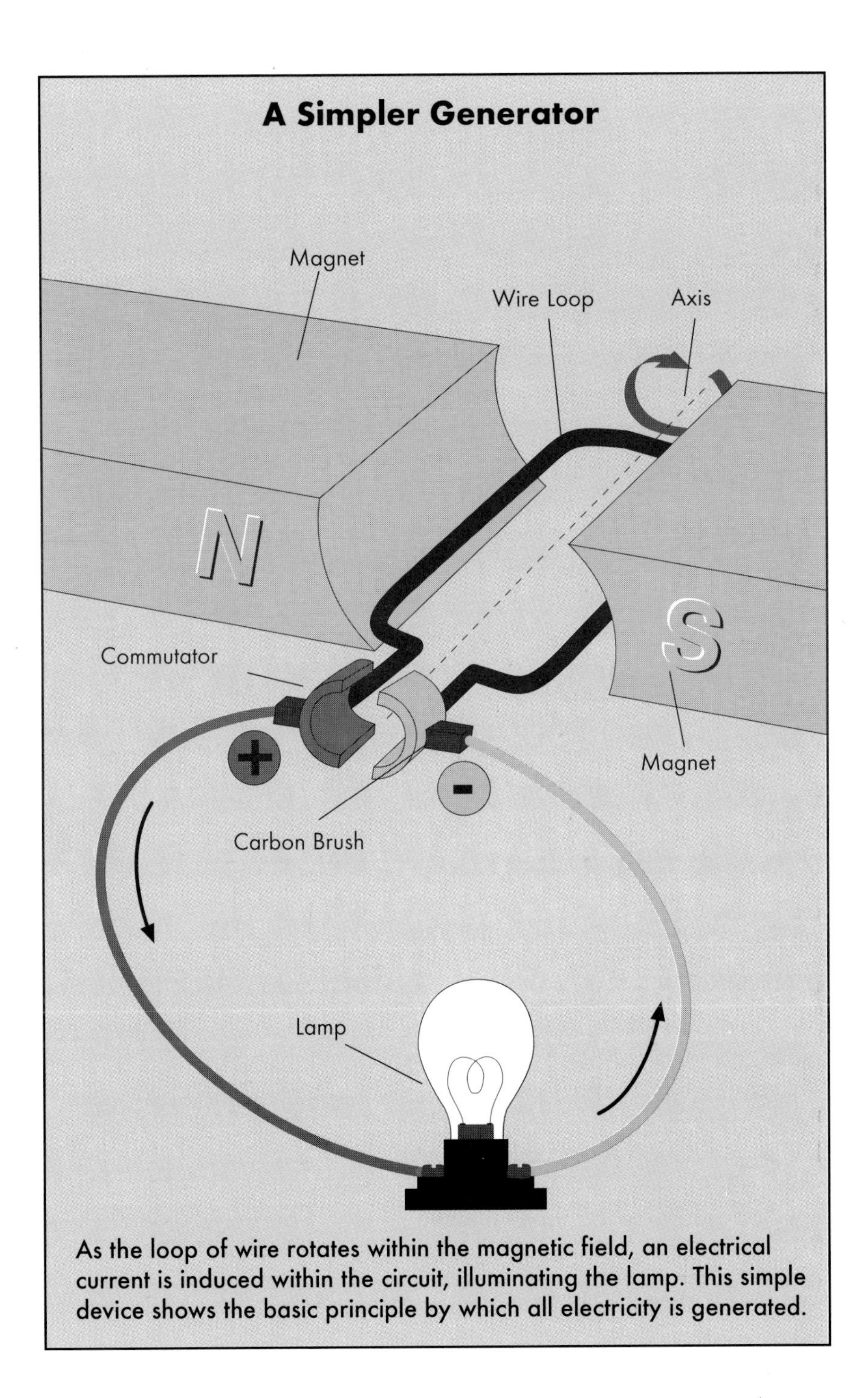

As the loop of wire rotates within the magnetic field, an electrical current is induced within the circuit, illuminating the lamp. This simple device shows the basic principle by which all electricity is generated.

Two Kinds of Current

The terms *alternating current* (AC) and *direct current* (DC) are familiar to most people. Radios, televisions, and most other appliances run on household current, which is alternating current. Batteries, whether they are in a car, a portable recorder, or a flashlight, deliver direct current. But what do these terms mean?

One of the most important parts of a dynamo is the magnet. Whether it is a permanent magnet or an electromagnet (a piece of metal that is magnetized only when an electric current runs through it), it has a magnetic field, with a north and a south pole. The other major part is the armature, a metal bar or disk wrapped with wire that rotates between the two poles of the magnet. In the early days, the armature was pushed along by steam; today, diesel or electric power moves it. As the armature travels past one of the magnet's poles, it cuts across the magnetic field, inducing a current. As it moves on, the current dies down. (If you were to make a graph representing the strength of the current, it would look like an upside-down U.)

As the armature approaches the magnet's other pole, it again cuts across the magnetic field, inducing an electrical current in the other

machine that could be connected to the current and turn it into usable energy. Such machines are known as generators, or dynamos. The first practical dynamo was patented 25 years later, in 1856.

Between the 1830s and the 1870s, many inventors tried to build motors powered by electrical current. Most of them used principles and designs that were borrowed from motors driven by steam. These motors, however, were often expensive to run and not very efficient. That is, electric-current motors did not do enough work to justify the energy required to run them.

direction. In this way, the direction of the current alternates as the armature turns. Each back-and-forth pair is called a cycle. The type of current produced is called alternating current.

A picture of the current's cycles would look like a line of inverted U's, with peaks and valleys representing surges of current that gradually ebb to a dead spot and then rise until they peak again.

Alternating current is the way electricity flows if nothing is done to alter the back-and-forth motion caused by the magnet's opposite poles. But a device called a commutator can be added to the dynamo to prevent the current from reversing directions. The current flows instead in the same direction always, rather than cycling back and forth. There are no cycles, and there are no peaks and valleys. The type of current produced in this case is called direct current.

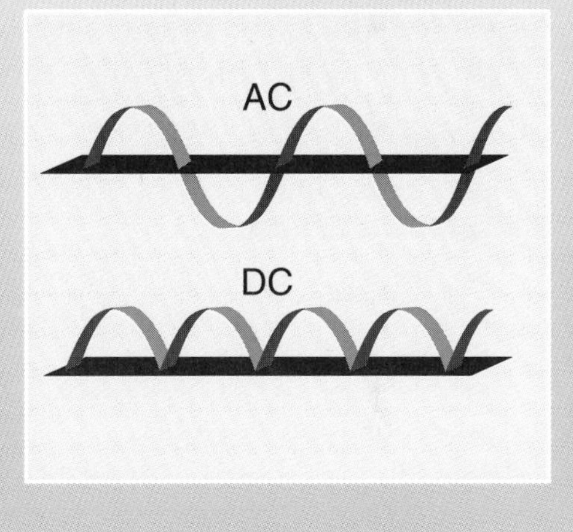

The Next Step

One of Michael Faraday's experiments provided an important clue to a way of producing more energy. Faraday knew that an electrical current could be passed from one coiled wire to another. If the sending, or primary, coil had fewer windings than the receiving, or secondary, coil, then the voltage, or power, of the electrical current would be increased. If the primary coil had more windings than the secondary coil did, the voltage would be decreased. Such a device is called a transformer, and the increase and decrease in voltage are called stepping up and stepping down.

Moving a current from a primary coil with very few windings to a secondary one with many more windings made it possible to step up the voltage dramatically. This could be done in a series of steps, with increasingly greater numbers of windings. The result could be extremely high-voltage electrical currents.

Faraday's transformer and all those that came after it depended on there being a varying magnetic field. That exists only with alternating current—AC—and not with direct current—DC (see page 55). As a result, the only kind of electricity that can be stepped up or stepped down is alternating current.

The range of direct current voltage is very narrow. In contrast, alternating current voltage can be stepped up to extremely high levels or stepped down to levels comparable to those of direct current.

It is this fact that made all the difference in what was to follow. One point of view was that the high voltages possible with alternating current made it a force too dangerous for widespread use. Another was that alternating current was a powerful source of energy that could be tamed to serve the public.

Delivering Electricity

It is one thing to generate electricity. It is quite another to transport it. Moving electricity from its source to where it will be used depends on principles similar to those for moving a liquid or a gas.

A container that extends from the source of electricity to the point of use is needed to keep the substance together and moving in the intended direction. This is what is known as a conduit. Liquids and gases travel through pipes; electricity travels through wires.

It is pressure that moves the liquid, the gas, or the electricity along. Pressure is the result of one force pushing against another force that resists it. Liquid and gas pressure may exist naturally, or they may be produced artificially. For example, water cascading down a waterfall and natural gas released from inside the Earth are both pushed along by natural forces.

When water or gas is not under pressure, a pump can be used to produce pressure. Examples are water in a reservoir and illuminating gas manufactured by burning coal. George Westinghouse witnessed the awesome force of natural gas. Later on in his life, the power of the great Niagara Falls would also set him thinking about how to harness that energy.

In the case of electrical current, voltage can be thought of as pressure. The higher the voltage, the greater the pressure—and the farther and faster the current can move along the conduit. The transformer, then, is similar to the water or gas pump.

Direct current, on the other hand, is like a meandering river flowing over level ground. It has low voltage, which means it has very little pressure. It gradually loses its power as it flows. Because nothing can be done to "step up," or increase, that power, direct-current generators have to be located very close to where the electricity will actually be used. Practically speaking, direct current can be delivered no farther than a mile from its source. Alternating current, however, can be stepped up to very high voltages; thus, it can travel distances of many miles. As a result, alternating-current generators can be located outside of populated areas. Electricity can then be transported to large cities or can be shared by several small towns. It can even be delivered to remote rural areas.

Spotlight on Thomas Edison

In the United States, the name that is perhaps most closely associated with electricity is that of Thomas Alva Edison. By the 1870s, he had already made a name for himself as the inventor of the phonograph. He patented his electric light in 1879 and then set about finding a way to supply the power to run it.

Edison had a master plan: He wanted to sell lightbulbs, of course, but he intended to be the sole supplier of everything involved with making them glow. In the early days, his customers were limited to those who could afford generators: rich people, banks, hotels, and prosperous businesses. Expanding his operation meant getting electricity to more people.

In 1882, Thomas Edison's Electric Light Company opened the first electrical-power generating station, on Pearl Street in downtown New York City. Because it was delivering direct current, the area that it supplied was relatively small—one square mile south of Fulton Street. Edison's idea was to build many generating stations to serve different neighborhoods. By 1887, there were 121 Edison electrical-power generating stations in operation or being built in the United States and Europe. Edison had pinned his hopes on direct current, and he was determined to build an empire based on it.

Thomas Edison stands in his Orange, New Jersey, laboratory, where many of his great inventions were developed.

Westinghouse Gets to Work

Meanwhile, back in Pittsburgh, Westinghouse was thinking about electricity, too. To his mind, alternating current was the wave of the future. Westinghouse was especially interested in work that was going on in Europe to build motors and transformers that ran on alternating current.

Westinghouse's involvement in the development of electrical power marked a change in his way of working. Whereas he had previously used his own ideas to create a product, he now put together a team of experts and financed their explorations in this new field.

Nonetheless, he remained involved in day-to-day operations, as biographer Henry G. Prout wrote in 1922:

> *Those who watched Westinghouse and worked with him through the years ceased to be surprised at his capacity to do extraordinary things and do them quickly. They learned, too, that this capacity was not only a matter of intellectual gifts, but also a matter of dogged industry and of power to work fast and make other men work fast. Through the long evenings he worked in his private [railroad] car and in his house, designing, sketching, and dictating. In his car any corner of a table would do, in his house he worked on a billiard table. Seated and leaning uncomfortably over the rail, he drew rapidly and with accuracy and completeness of detail, while those around him watched and answered questions and made suggestions if they could. Probably he had no pencil but borrowed one from the nearest man. As these pencils were never returned one wondered what became of them. His trail through the world was blazed with other men's pencils.*

The Engine of Progress

Among Westinghouse's employees at the Union Switch and Signal Company were a number of talented young electrical engineers. Three of them, Guido Pantaleoni, William Stanley, and Reginald Belfield, made important contributions to the new world of alternating current.

While on a trip to his native Italy in 1885, Pantaleoni sent Westinghouse an exciting cable. From a former teacher, he had learned about a transformer that had been designed by a Frenchman named Lucien Gaulard and an Englishman named John Dixon Gibbs. Westinghouse realized that the device would be a valuable addition to the alternating current system that he was developing. Thus, he directed Pantaleoni to buy the license for the Gaulard and Gibbs transformer.

The transformer itself was brought to Pittsburgh by Belfield, who was an assistant to Gaulard and Gibbs. Belfield also brought a prototype AC generator, which had been designed by the German electrical engineer Werner von Siemens. After examining the transformer, Westinghouse concluded that it was a crude device, ill suited to large-scale commercial use. He assigned Stanley and Belfield the task of redesigning the transformer for that purpose.

Westinghouse Electric Is Born

Westinghouse knew that harnessing electricity would be a far more ambitious undertaking than designing brake and signal systems for railroads. As had become his habit, Westinghouse set up a company for his newest venture.

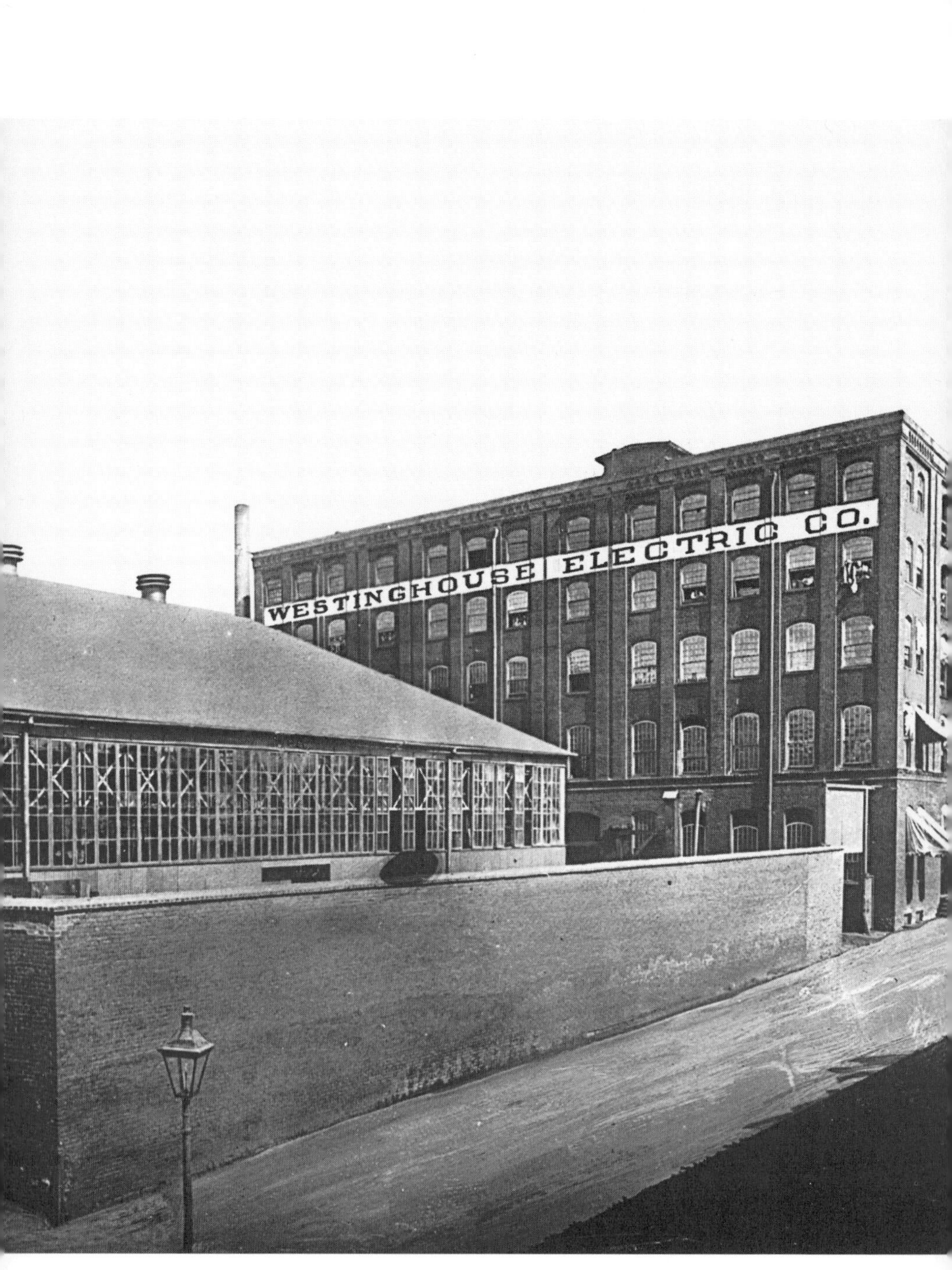

This rented plant on the Allegheny River was the first home of the Westinghouse Electric Company when it was chartered on January 8, 1886, to produce electrical equipment.

In January 1886, the Westinghouse Electric Company was founded to, in the words of its charter, "manufacture and promote the use of alternating current system equipment." George Westinghouse was its president. His youngest brother, Herman, was its vice president. The company was housed in the original Union Switch and Signal Company factory, which had by then moved to larger quarters.

While Stanley and Belfield were working on their part of the project, Stanley became ill and had to return to his home in Great Barrington, Massachusetts. Reluctant to lose a valued employee and to interrupt important work, Westinghouse sent Belfield to join him and paid for the two men to continue their work in Stanley's hometown. The investment paid off within a few short months.

The Lights Go On in New England

Great Barrington is nestled in the Berkshire Mountains. In 1886, it was a sleepy town boasting a business district with 13 stores, two hotels, two doctor's offices, a telephone exchange, and a post office.

Stanley and Belfield set themselves up in an abandoned mill just outside of town. A 25-horsepower steam engine was hooked up to the Siemens alternating current generator. The generator, in turn, was attached to the redesigned transformer, which would step up the current produced by the generator. Wires attached to trees and leading to the buildings on Main Street were strung into the center of town. Outside the buildings were other transformers to step down the current before it traveled to the lamps inside. The lamps ranged in size from 16 to 150 candlepower, a measure that compared their brightness to the light given off by the number of burning candles indicated.

On March 20, 1886, Stanley threw the switch in his workshop three-quarters of a mile away, and the tiny village lit up under the nighttime sky. Stanley later said that it was a festive night. People crowded the streets and stores. Though wary of the lights, they celebrated the accomplishment. This first demonstration in the United States of alternating current transmission was a small but important beginning.

Shortly afterward, Stanley sent his current as far as the town of Lawrenceville, four miles away, and kept 400 lamps burning for two weeks. The Westinghouse alternating current system was ready to be presented publicly, and, before long, orders for citywide installations came in. The first was from Buffalo, New York, which was "lit up" in November 1886. By the end of the year, Westinghouse Electric had received 27 orders. Within four years, the company would install 300 central power stations supplying alternating current to the cities and towns of America.

Enter Nikola Tesla

Nikola Tesla could have been cast in the movie role of the mad scientist. A highly eccentric man, he was born in 1856 in Smiljan, Croatia, a part of the former Yugoslavia that today is again an independent state. He was in many ways the polar opposite of George Westinghouse.

Westinghouse considered Tesla to be a theoretical genius. Ideas poured fast and furiously into Tesla's mind, but he was rarely able to turn them into practical products. Whereas Westinghouse developed his ideas through

Nikola Tesla was a brilliant scientist, but he didn't have as much commercial success as either Westinghouse or Edison.

painstaking hours of drawing and making models, Tesla's came to him as fully formed visions. Unlike Westinghouse, who made the most of collaborations with other people, Tesla was not a team player. He found it difficult to get along with others and preferred to work on his own. Rather than taking advantage of the protection provided by the patent laws, it was he who was often taken advantage of.

The earliest electrical induction (creation) motors generated a direct current because of a device called a commutator, which was part of the design. Now, the search was on for a way to create alternating current. Although making an alternating current motor was more complicated than simply eliminating the commutator, Tesla managed to do so, in 1881. According to one account, while walking in a park one day, Tesla fell into a trancelike state. When he regained full consciousness, the concept and the design for the alternating current induction motor were in his mind and, with a stick, he quickly drew a picture of it in the dirt.

He built his first one two years later. By then he had moved to Paris to work for the Continental Edison Company. In 1884, he came to America and began working for Thomas Edison himself. Edison was interested in Tesla's design because he was eager to develop a similar motor. In Edison's opinion, however, it had to use direct current. The two men quickly clashed. Edison was firm in his conviction that direct current was the most effective way to supply electricity to homes and industry. But Tesla, like Westinghouse, believed that alternating current was the only sensible approach.

After a year of battling over the issue, Edison and Tesla parted company. Tesla insisted that he had been cheated out of money. He said that he had designed 24 different types of machines with the understanding that Edison would pay Tesla $50,000 upon their completion. However, according to Tesla, this reward never materialized. He resigned his position.

Tesla moved to New York City and set up an independent laboratory. He believed that until a way could be found to eliminate the peaks and valleys of alternating current cycles, a smooth flow of electrical power would not be possible. He went to work on overcoming that obstacle.

Tesla's answer was to generate three upside-down U's that would overlap. With three cycles that begin and end at different times, there is always one cycle nearing its peak. The timing of cycles is called an interval, or phase. Tesla called his device a polyphase generator. (*Poly* is the Greek word for "several.")

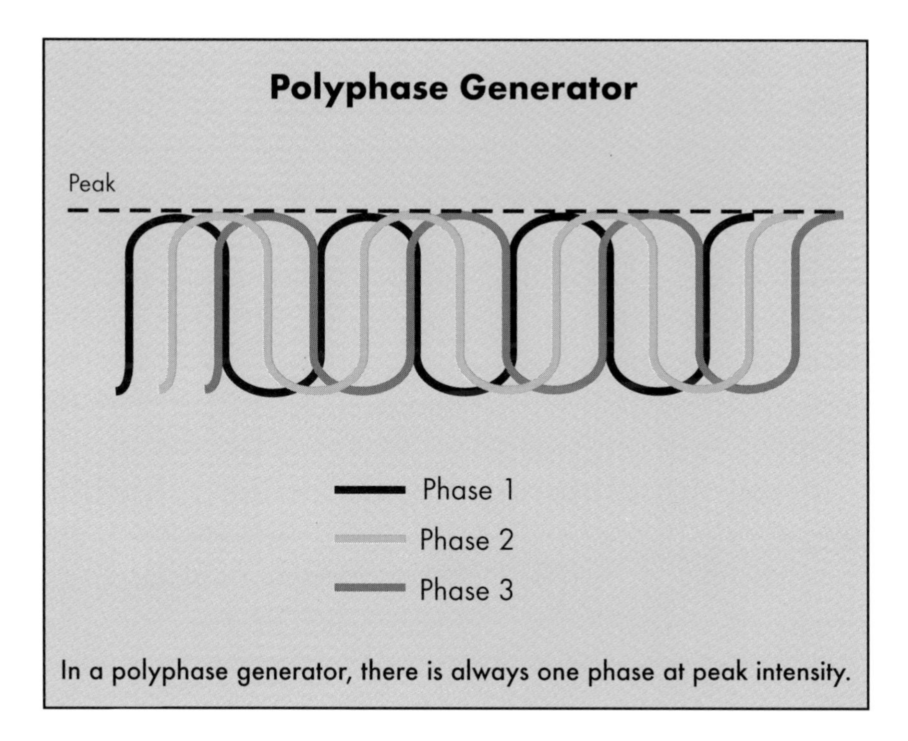

In a polyphase generator, there is always one phase at peak intensity.

In May 1888, Tesla presented a speech, "New System of Alternate Current Motors and Transformers," before the American Institute of Electrical Engineers. When Westinghouse learned of Tesla's work, he summoned him to Pittsburgh. He paid Tesla the enormous sum of $2,000 a month and an additional amount for the right to use his polyphase motor in his own products and services.

Not surprisingly, Nikola Tesla's defection to the Westinghouse camp infuriated Thomas Edison. Edison viewed Westinghouse as the enemy and took Tesla's leaving as a personal insult. In fact, Edison was itching for a fight.

Genius at Work

Tesla's alternating current motor was, of course, not the only version around. The Siemens generator that was used in Westinghouse's commercial installations worked adequately, but it had its problems. It was a single-phase generator, so lags and surges of power were unavoidable. Tesla's polyphase generator solved those problems, but it could not be connected to the Westinghouse system without modifications. The reason was that all the components of the Westinghouse system used electric current running at a frequency, or speed, of 133 Hz (hertz, or cycles per second), whereas Tesla's generator delivered it at 60 Hz.

George Westinghouse set Tesla to work on modifying his invention so that it would match the 133-Hz standard. He reasoned that it would be easier, cheaper, and faster to change one part of the system rather than many.

As it turns out, Westinghouse was wrong—and he learned an expensive lesson in the process. After three years of work,

Postscript on Nikola Tesla

After leaving Westinghouse Electric, Nikola Tesla returned to New York and worked on many other groundbreaking ideas in the field of electricity. One of them involved using radio waves for long-distance wireless communication.

In 1915, the Italian inventor Guglielmo Marconi tried to patent a wide range of devices and processes related to radio communications. Tesla objected, saying that most of Marconi's claims were based on ideas he had come up with first, many of which he had patented. The U.S. Patent Office disagreed with Tesla and granted the patents to Marconi. It was not until 1943, the year of Tesla's death, that the decision was reversed. It is Marconi, however, who won a Nobel Prize for his work on radiotelegraphy and he who is remembered by history as the inventor of the radio.

That, in many ways, was the story of Tesla's life. He died in New York in 1943, at the age of 87, a recluse and a bitter man.

Westinghouse researchers had concluded that a frequency of 133 Hz did not work for alternating current motors.

Tesla did his best, but after working on the project for four years, he concluded that the goal was impossible to achieve. Westinghouse saw the light and agreed to change all the other components of the system—and the frequency for alternating current—to 60 Hz. This frequency remains the standard today.

By the time that challenge had been met, Tesla and Westinghouse parted ways. Tesla, who was uncomfortable working as part of a team, was eager to return to his own laboratory and his experiments. All the same, their collaboration ended amicably, without the anger and mutual feelings of betrayal that seemed to mark Tesla's break with Thomas Edison.

In contrast to his bitter words about Edison, Tesla praised Westinghouse in this way:

> *George Westinghouse was, in my opinion, the only man on this globe who could take my alternating current system under the circumstances then existing and win the battle against prejudice and money power. He was one of the world's true noblemen, of whom America may well be proud and to whom humanity owes an immense debt of gratitude.*

Even though Nikola Tesla no longer worked for Westinghouse, his patents did. Westinghouse had bought the rights to 40 of Tesla's patents, including those for the polyphase motor and for a transformer popularly known as the Tesla coil. As a result, he was able to use them in future projects. Westinghouse had made a generous deal with Tesla: He paid Tesla a royalty every time his inventions were used. It is clear that two ventures that put Westinghouse Electric on the map relied heavily on Tesla's work—lighting the Columbian Exposition and harnessing Niagara Falls.

It is ironic that Nikola Tesla was the link between George Westinghouse and Thomas Edison, the two men who engineered the American electrical revolution, because it was his devices that became the principal weapons in the clash of titans that was soon to come.

CHAPTER FIVE

Waging the Battle of the Currents

It may be easier to understand how important the contest between alternating and direct currents was if you compare it to the present-day contest between the operating systems of the Macintosh and Windows computers. Because the two operating systems are not compatible, a buyer has to choose one or the other. Both are backed by multibillion-dollar businesses, and each would like to be the system that everyone chooses. There are efforts under way to develop a means of making the systems compatible; in the meantime, however, the creators of the rival systems, and the computer companies that use them, continue to wage advertising and public-relations campaigns to convince consumers that their product is the best.

In the contest between alternating current and direct current, there was little chance of a team effort. Part of that had to do with the personalities of the men most closely identified with the two sides of the issue—George Westinghouse and Thomas Edison.

A Clash of Titans

Thomas Alva Edison is an American hero. There is no doubt, however, that he had a dark side. He could be abrasive and stubborn, even arrogant. He is famous for using other people's ideas and inventions without giving credit even to the loyal people who worked with him over the years. He was skillful at manipulating the press and public opinion to gain favor for his projects. In short, he hated to be wrong, and he hated to lose.

Edison was much better at raising money than his rival George Westinghouse. The Edison Electric Light Company was financed by the "big money" of the Vanderbilts and J. P. Morgan, powerful men who knew how to influence public opinion when it came to protecting their investments. In contrast, the agonizingly slow experiments taking place in Pittsburgh were draining Westinghouse Electric of needed funds. In time, that and other money problems would have a disastrous effect on Westinghouse—both the man and the company.

Edison first tried using scientific facts to defend direct current. He was unable to get around direct current's main disadvantage, however: There was no practical way to step up voltage and, therefore, no way to transmit it effectively over long distances.

His next effort was to attack alternating current as being too dangerous to be trusted. That meant launching a smear campaign, complete with dirty tricks and personal insults.

Edison focused his attack on what was known to be alternating current's greatest advantage: high voltage. There was no question that high-voltage electricity could kill, and what could be more "shocking" than to show people what that looked like?

In 1890, Edison and his supporters staged several public electrocution demonstrations to make their point. The first demonstration, given in Orange, New Jersey, involved stray dogs that had been rounded up for the purpose. Next, during a talk at the Columbia School of Mines, one of Edison's henchmen tortured and killed a large dog with alternating current. Only the intervention of the superintendent of the Society for the Prevention of Cruelty to Animals kept him from electrocuting a second victim. Edison had horses and cows electrocuted to show that living things even larger than human beings could be killed by high-voltage alternating current. It was cruel and horrible, and it definitely had the intended effect on public opinion.

George Westinghouse ignored these dramatic tactics, and continued to focus on research and development in his workshops. He was as concerned as everyone else about the dangers of high-voltage electricity, but he felt confident that underground cables and heavy insulation would provide sufficient protection for the public.

One of the dirtiest tricks played by the Edison camp involved the electric chair. In those days, executions were carried out by hanging, but there were many people who hoped to find a more humane way to put criminals to death. Suddenly, Edison began promoting the use of alternating

Edison, shown here, favored the use of electricity for execution. Westinghouse strongly opposed this idea.

current—as the best way to execute a condemned man. He even testified in court about its advantages.

Westinghouse refused to sell any equipment that might be used for such a purpose, so the Edison camp arranged, through a middleman, to buy a Westinghouse alternating current generator and have it installed in the death house of New York's Sing Sing prison. It was there, in August 1890, that the electric chair was first used to put someone to death. Witnesses reported that it was a gruesome affair, and *The New York Times* declared it "an awful spectacle, far worse than hanging."

The term *electrocution* had not yet been coined. In what Edison hoped would be the final blow, one of his supporters suggested that the term *westinghousing* be adopted for this mode of execution.

There is no evidence that Westinghouse joined the mud-slinging, although he knew that he faced a formidable foe. Fortunately, an opportunity to wage a fair fight presented itself just when things seemed most desperate.

The Columbian Exposition, a world's fair showcasing the latest technology, was scheduled to be held in Chicago in 1893. Organizers seeking to provide lighting for the vast fair-grounds asked for bids. Westinghouse Electric and Edison's company, by then called Edison General Electric, were among those that answered the challenge.

George Westinghouse knew that this would be the show-down. Chicago was Edison country—the capital city of the Midwest was lit by the Edison Electric Company. Westinghouse decided to make the most of the opportunity. He and his team figured out what kind of machinery they would need to provide the lighting and how much it would cost to do the job. The bid they came up with was much lower than Edison's, partly because Westinghouse did not build a profit into his prices. In his view, lighting the fair would be powerful advertising, and he was willing to break even or even lose money on the deal.

Westinghouse won the contract to light the world's fair just 11 months before opening day. There was a lot of work to be done and no time to lose. Almost immediately, however, Westinghouse encountered a huge obstacle. Thomas Edison's electric lamp was by far the best around, and he held a monopoly on its sale. He was not about to let his chief competitor use this valuable product. In 1892, Westinghouse took Edison to court for the right to buy the bulb. But at the same time, he assembled a special team and gave them a special assignment: to develop a new lamp that could be manufactured in large quantities for about a third of the price of Edison's.

The solution they came up with was called the stopper lamp, and it was based on a patent that Westinghouse had previously purchased. Although this bulb was not better than Edison's and was never any competition on the open market, it served the immediate purpose brilliantly. Edison's bulb consisted of a one-piece glass globe with a very thin piece of carbon, called a filament, inside. All air was removed from the globe, which allowed the filament to glow but not to burn up. The Westinghouse bulb consisted of two pieces: The first piece of the globe looked like a rounded bottle, and the second piece resembled a small cork, or stopper, inserted in the bottle's neck. It was not much of a difference, but it was enough to satisfy the patent authorities.

The two-piece construction made it harder to maintain a vacuum inside the globe. As a result, the stopper lamps burned out more quickly than Edison's bulbs did.

The illumination of the Columbian Exposition in 1893 was a major achievement for Westinghouse.

Westinghouse manufactured 250,000 stopper lamps so that there would be enough replacements to keep the fairgrounds brightly lit for the six-month duration of the Columbian Exposition. Thanks to Nikola Tesla, they were powered by twelve 75-ton polyphase generators.

Victory in the White City

The battle for the contract to illuminate the Columbian Exposition was fitting, because the world's fair itself showcased, as no other event could, the power of electricity and its growing importance in American life.

The Westinghouse central power station was capable of lighting 172,000 16-candlepower lamps at one time. In addition to its illumination of the entire fairgrounds, the Westinghouse Electric Company had a stunning exhibit in Machinery Hall. Models of Tesla's motor and numerous demonstrations of the safety of alternating current were among the highlights. The exhibit even included a rotary converter that could change alternating to direct current.

Exhibitors at the fair from 72 countries gave the more than 27 million visitors a glimpse of the future. Among the exciting exhibits were an Eastman camera and a gasoline-powered Benz motorcar. The biggest crowd pleaser was the world's first Ferris wheel, a mammoth structure that could hold more than 2,000 people at a time and that offered a breathtaking view of the fairgrounds.

Thomas Edison was there, too, showing off his phonograph, a talking doll, and an electric railway, all brilliantly illuminated among other inventions by his own electric lights. Even so, there was no question that Westinghouse had won the day. The beauty and the excitement of what was popularly called the White City was there for all the world to see. George Westinghouse had proved that alternating current worked, that it was safe and economical, and that it could improve everyday life.

Harnessing the Falls

Three years before the Columbian Exposition opened, an international commission had been put together to study the possibility of using the great falls of the Niagara River to generate power on a large scale.

Headed by the English physicist Lord William Kelvin, the commission had remained divided on the issue of which type of current to use. The triumphant show of alternating current power in Chicago tipped the balance. In view of the Westinghouse system's ability to deliver current over long distances—and to do so safely—the commission awarded the contract to Westinghouse Electric in October 1893, just days before the Columbian Exposition ended.

If George Westinghouse had gambled that the Columbian Exposition would show the world that alternating current was far superior to anything else, the payoff came with the Niagara Falls project. This was the height of the "battle of the currents," as it represented the largest electrical project ever undertaken. The country would likely follow its lead in its use of either alternating or direct current. Whichever way the falls went, the nation would go.

The power station would be built by the Cataract Construction Company, and the machinery would be supplied by Westinghouse Electric. At the heart of the system

English physicist Lord Kelvin (right) stands with George Westinghouse.

were Nikola Tesla's polyphase induction motor and the improved Gaulard and Gibbs transformer.

The initial order called for Westinghouse to deliver three 5,000-horsepower dynamos. The first one was installed within 18 months. By November 1895, all three were in place. The first city to benefit was Buffalo, New York, 22 miles away. Eventually, ten Westinghouse generators were installed in the Niagara station. This additional power changed the face of the region.

Money Trouble

Throughout the nineteenth century, the American economy experienced periodic financial crises. These so-called panics occurred when people lost confidence in the stability of the banks and in the value of money. Most large businesses relied on money loaned by banks and private investors. In times of panic, they were particularly vulnerable. Many banks and businesses collapsed during panics, throwing untold numbers of workers out of their jobs.

Large-scale financial panics occurred three times before the Civil War and four more times before World War I. One of those panics took place in 1893, when Westinghouse was putting on his dramatic show in Chicago. Between the expensive years with Tesla and the all-out effort to light the Columbian Exposition, he had borrowed a lot of money. (His plan was to win approval, not to make a profit, in the White City.) The Panic of 1893 left Westinghouse Electric Company on financially shaky ground.

Another financial panic occurred in 1907, and that one brought the wobbling company to its knees.

The Power of Falling Water

The concept of hydroelectric power, or using the energy in falling water to run electrical generators, was relatively new in 1893. A few hydroelectric plants had been built in Europe, and Westinghouse had built three in the United States.

However, nothing in the world had been conceived on the scale of the project at the huge Niagara Falls, which plummets nearly 170 feet into a gorge at the boundary of the U.S. and Canada.

Hydroelectric power is an important source of renewable energy. That is, unlike such fuel sources as wood, coal, and oil, it is not used up in the course of producing energy; water is here to stay.

Falling water exists naturally or it can be manufactured. If no waterfall exists in a particular area, a dam can be built across a river.

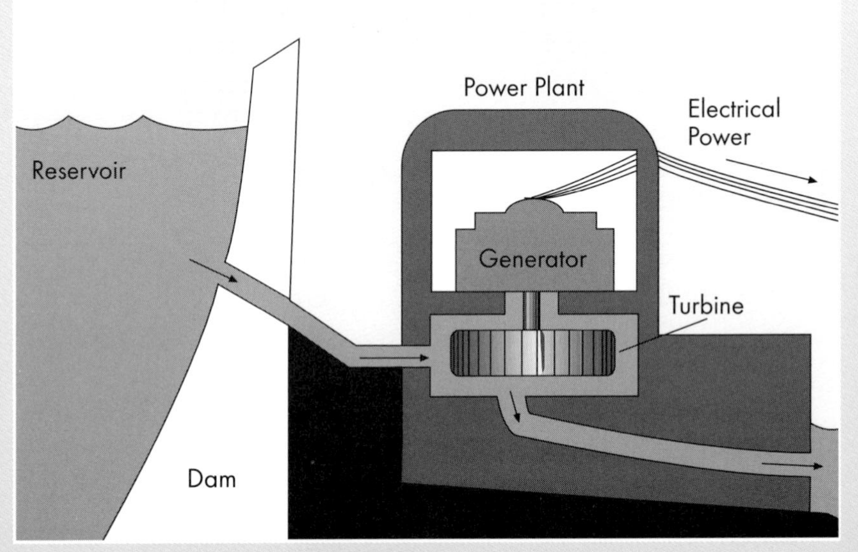

Force from water released through a dam drives turbines, which produce electricity.

Enormous energy builds up as the flow of the river is held back by the dam. The energy is then tapped when the water is released to drive the generators.

Hydroelectric-power plants supply about 25 percent of the electricity used in the world today. One of the greatest is that of Aswan High Dam in Egypt, which was completed in 1970. Using the power of the Nile River, it supplies as much as a quarter of the electricity used in that desert country. In the United States, the golden age of dam building in the 1930s gave us the vast chain in the Tennessee Valley, the Hoover Dam built on the Colorado River, and the Grand Coulee Dam across the Columbia River in Washington State. The last two are equipped with Westinghouse machines.

An interior view of one of the Niagara Falls powerhouses shows the 5,000 horsepower dynamos, switches, and switch control board.

Threatened with bankruptcy, the Westinghouse Electric Company was taken over by a new board of directors. One of their first acts was to remove George Westinghouse as president. Their job was to turn the company around, and they considered Westinghouse to be a poor financial manager who would stand in the way of that effort.

It is true that Westinghouse was a great gambler, interested more in products than in profits. He was notorious for pouring whatever money the company earned into the development of new projects. Now that reputation had come back to haunt him.

George Westinghouse was crushed by this disastrous turn of events. By 1911, he had severed all connections with Westinghouse Electric Company, although it continued to bear his name and does to this day. Instead, he turned his attention to other inventions, returning to his air-brake and switch-and-signal companies, both of which had survived the panic.

The Unstoppable Mr. Westinghouse

If you are imagining a defeated general retreating into obscurity, think again. The powerful industrialist Andrew Carnegie himself said, "George Westinghouse is a man who can't be downed." In the years following 1907, some 60 patents were registered in Westinghouse's name. He started several companies and branched out into new fields, such as the automobile and oceangoing steamship industries.

There is a kind of justice in the fact that Westinghouse's last great undertaking was an echo of his first. It is as though his life had come full circle.

One happy occasion during a difficult period for Westinghouse was the 1909 wedding in England of his son George III and Violet Brocklebank.

Owing to the success of the Niagara Falls project, many other regions of the country wanted alternating current generating stations as well. As none of these regions contained a waterfall massive enough to turn the generators, however, another primary source of power was needed. (America's huge dam-building projects of the New Deal era were still more than a quarter century in the future.)

George Westinghouse had never stopped being intrigued by the possibilities of the rotary engine. His interest was sparked anew when he learned that an English inventor named Charles A. Parsons had built a powerful rotary steam engine, now called a turbine, and had successfully tested it on a ship called the *Turbinia*. Westinghouse bought exclusive American rights to the Parsons turbine in 1895. Working with Benjamin Lamme, another of his talented engineers, Westinghouse adapted the turbine for nonmarine use and installed three steam turbines in his air-brake plant. These were the first alternating-current steam turbines ever used in the United States.

In 1900, Westinghouse and Lamme built a huge turboalternator (an alternating current generator driven by a turbine) for the Hartford Electric Light Company in Connecticut. It was the first in the country used by a utility to manufacture power for its customers and was by far the most powerful turbine in the world.

Inspired by the success of the Hartford turboalternator and by Parsons's previous experience with the *Turbinia*, George Westinghouse next put his mind to marine uses of the turbine. It occurred to him that its rotary motion was suited far better to turning a ship's propeller than were the reciprocating engines then in use. Not only did the back-and-forth motion of a reciprocating engine have to be converted to rotary motion in order to turn the propeller, but such engines took up an enormous amount of space. They were also extremely noisy and created excessive vibration. All of these characteristics made a reciprocating engine an extremely undesirable choice in the cramped confines of a ship's engine room.

There was one problem that seemed insurmountable, however: A rotary engine operates most efficiently at high speed, whereas a propeller requires relatively low speed. Westinghouse enlisted the help of two marine engineers, George W. Melville and John H. McAlpine. Together they developed a reduction gear drive, which was able to transfer the power of the turbine to the propeller at the most useful speed without losing energy.

In 1912, a full 43 years after young George Westinghouse went begging to find a railroad willing to give his air brake a trial run, the United States Navy launched the U.S.S. *Neptune.* It was equipped with the Westinghouse turbine-and-gear combination. Its trial run was a great success, and his efficient turbine soon began to replace reciprocating engines on ships. As a Westinghouse Electric Company publication later noted, "It was a grand fulfillment, near the end of his life, of a development Westinghouse had envisioned almost half a century before."

Although Westinghouse had always enjoyed robust health, he developed heart trouble in 1913. His doctor ordered him to slow down and rest—a notion totally foreign to George Westinghouse. Nevertheless, he retired with Marguerite to Erskine Park, their grand estate in the Berkshire village of Lenox, Massachusetts. Shortly afterward, he caught a cold, which, in his weakened condition, he was unable to shake.

A Man of Honors

One of George Westinghouse's biographers once figured out that George spent a total of only one and a half years in school after the age of 13. Nonetheless, Westinghouse was showered with medals and honorary degrees, including a doctorate degree from Union College in Schenectady, where he had been a student for three short months.

He was elected president of the American Society of Mechanical Engineers in 1910. He received the Benjamin Franklin medal for his air brake and was inducted into both the National Inventors Hall of Fame and the Engineering and Science Hall of Fame. In 1955, Westinghouse was enshrined in the prestigious Hall of Fame of Great Americans at New York University.

He was an honorary member of the American Society for the Advancement of Science. His fame was not confined to the United States, however. Westinghouse received medals from France's Legion of Honor, Italy's Order of the Crown, and Belgium's Order of Leopold. However, perhaps his greatest–and most ironic–honor came in 1912, when he was awarded the Edison Gold Medal of the American Society of Electrical Engineers for championing alternating current.

In the late winter of 1914, Westinghouse and his wife decided that they should go to their home on Dupont Circle in Washington, D.C. Train travel in those days was still a bit rough—especially for a sick man—so the doctor suggested they make the trip in two stages, staying for a few days in a New York hotel where they kept a suite of rooms. At the hotel, even though he was a very sick man and confined to a wheelchair, Westinghouse's inventive spirit was as strong as ever. He now worked on designs for an electrically operated wheelchair. On the morning of March 12, 1914, he died while sitting in his wheelchair. His designs were nearby. He was 67 years old.

He left behind a world very different from the one into which he was born. In his lifetime, George Westinghouse witnessed the growth of the United States as the world's greatest industrial power. In a very real sense, he was among the giants who made it happen.

CHAPTER SIX

The Westinghouse Legacy

George Westinghouse, the temperamental boy who would not take "no" for an answer, became one of the most important figures in the creation of industrial America. Unlike his fellow inventor Nikola Tesla, Westinghouse was able to turn his ideas into marketable products that transformed the lives of people the world over. And unlike his bitter rival, Thomas Edison, he is remembered not only as a brilliant man but also as a kind one.

Nearly 100 years after his death, George Westinghouse's name and work are still alive. It is no surprise that he is still associated with a broad range of contemporary industries

The technological achievement of night illumination was a development that transformed people's lives.

and endeavors at the end of the twentieth century, just as he was at the beginning of it.

Henry G. Prout, who was one of Westinghouse's biographers, and had known the man personally, described him in heroic terms:

> *In the manufacture of power, as in the development of transportation, George Westinghouse stands amongst the apostles of democracy. He invented and caused other men to invent. He created companies and built factories in many countries. He organized, stimulated, and guided the activities of scores of thousands. . . . He did more, far more, for the foundation of that development than any other man who ever lived. Into it entered his imagination, his courage, and his tenacity in greater measure perhaps than into any other of his deeds.*

A Man of Character

An explanation for George Westinghouse's enduring presence can be found by examining the kind of person that he was. The pioneering British physicist Lord Kelvin, a contemporary and colleague of Westinghouse, said, "George Westinghouse is in character and achievements one of the great men of our time." Throughout his long life, Westinghouse's fine spirit and strong character would help him to overcome many challenges and to win the loyalty and support of his workers.

One of his greatest gifts was his ability to build on and recycle ideas. If an idea was not right for a project he was working on, he did not discard it. He simply filed it away for future reference, for a time when the idea might work. The

The inventions of George Westinghouse (left) still affect the lives of people around the world.

rotary engine that he patented at age 19 was never manufactured, but he took advantage of the principles he discovered in designing it when, at age 54, he installed the turboalternator that brought alternating current power to Hartford, Connecticut. Ideas that did work were often adapted to other uses. He took what he had learned about pneumatic pressure valves while perfecting his air brake to design safety valves in his natural-gas pipe systems. What he had learned about transporting natural gas under enormous pressure, then reducing the pressure at its point of use, came in handy when he was trying to figure out how to transport high-voltage electrical power and safely step it down for home use.

This sort of resourcefulness served Westinghouse well throughout his career. People who worked with him marveled at his ability to persevere in solving a problem; if one approach did not work, Westinghouse would quickly try another, and another, until he found a solution. One man who knew him likened Westinghouse's brain to a "storehouse of original ideas."

As becomes apparent over and over again in the story of his life, George Westinghouse was always questioning, and always curious. There is no doubt that much of Westinghouse's success was the result of hard work, commitment, and persistence. He simply would not give up on an idea or a project if he thought it was a good one. Perhaps what was regarded as stubbornness in him as a child developed into tenacity as an adult. Westinghouse said something like that himself when, as an older man, he observed that he had always been good at getting what he wanted. But what he got through tantrums as a child, he got through hard work as an adult.

Another of his gifts was his ability to follow through from idea to product. There are many examples of this pattern, whether in transportation or energy technology. First he would see a need, often before other people did. Next he would figure out an approach to filling that need, which led to an invention, often after a painstaking process of trial and error. Finally, he would set up a company to turn that invention into a product and to manufacture and market it.

But perhaps his greatest gift was his willingness to work with others. George Westinghouse was a man who liked to share ideas. He always shared credit, and he believed in rewarding talent and paying for the efforts of others. The name Westinghouse is associated with some of the greatest inventive minds of the time: Tesla, Stanley, Lamme, and many others. In fact, it was Tesla who pointed out that Westinghouse was rigorously conscientious in respecting other people's intellectual property. If Westinghouse did use other people's ideas and inventions, he had acquired them fairly. This principle governed his treatment of all of his employees. And today it is still responsible for the nurturing of scientific talent done by the Westinghouse Electric Corporation.

Although Westinghouse no longer manufactures consumer products, many people remember the Westinghouse refrigerators and washing machines and other labor-saving devices, with which many Americans grew up.

A Vast Influence

The next time you are on a train about to move out of the railroad station, listen for a hissing noise. That sound, the hallmark of a Westinghouse air brake, tells you that as you

Generations of Americans have fond memories of Westinghouse refrigerators and other electric household appliances made possible by alternating current.

travel toward your destination, any stops that the train makes along the way will be both safe and gentle. Even though much has changed about passenger and freight travel in the years since George Westinghouse perfected the air brake, most trains today still use brakes made according to his design.

If you are planning to take a cross-country trip by train, a look at a map showing you all the available rail routes should also remind you of George Westinghouse. Without Westinghouse's innovative system of automatic train switches and signals, the vast network of railroad lines that spans the North American continent would not have been possible.

You do not have to leave home, however, to benefit from the Westinghouse legacy. Every time you plug in an electrical appliance, switch on a television set, or turn on a light, you are tapping into the alternating current that Westinghouse brought to American homes. If the electricity in your area is generated by hydroelectric power, chances are good that the turbines at the power station are descended from those that Westinghouse installed at Niagara Falls. If you live in the West, your power may come directly from the generators that Westinghouse Electric Corporation built at the Hoover Dam and the Grand Coulee Dam in the 1930s and 1940s.

Whether you have a gas range or an electric stove in your kitchen, you may be reminded of Westinghouse every time you cook a meal or bake a cake. Natural gas, which heats many American homes and fuels many gas stoves, is an abundant natural resource. Piping natural gas through communities, however, would not be safe had it not been for George Westinghouse.

Westinghouse was responsible for harnessing the hydropower of the great Niagara River.

Improving Employee Life

Toward the end of his life, George Westinghouse said, "If someday they say of me that in my work I have contributed something to the welfare and happiness of my fellow men, I shall be satisfied." His sense of responsibility extended beyond the technological advances in which he played so large a part.

The history of industrialization is filled with tales of human misery. As much as industrial progress has bettered the lives of people, it has also created working and environmental conditions that have harmed them. Factory towns and the pollution they engender often represent the dark side of the story.

George Westinghouse was aware of this as he watched Pittsburgh mushroom into a major industrial center, partly because of the growth of his own companies. He knew that working people and their families often lived in squalor and that their health and education were badly in need of improvement. He believed that he had a moral responsibility as well as the financial resources to do something about these problems.

In 1871, Westinghouse instituted Saturday "half holidays" for all his employees. Amazing as it may seem today, then, the American workweek was six days long, there were no guaranteed vacations. Remembering a promise he had made to himself as a teenager working in his father's shop, he closed down his factories on Saturday afternoons, a practice that had to be followed by other companies in the Pittsburgh area and throughout the United States. Company-sponsored picnics and outings lightened the burden for many. In the

1880s, Westinghouse added vacations with pay to employee benefits.

In 1889, ground was broken for a model factory town in Turtle Creek Valley, 14 miles east of Pittsburgh. In the town now called Wilmerding, Westinghouse built affordable housing for his workers, with indoor toilets and plumbing and electric and natural-gas outlets with which to light and heat the homes. Most of the homes had lawns and gardens, and the company held contests in which cash prizes were awarded to those with the most beautiful gardens. The small town soon became a center of good taste in the region. The community, to which he moved the air-brake plant in 1890, also had a hospital and schools for the children of his workers. In 1907, a Welfare Building was added. It contained a gym, a pool, classrooms, reading rooms, and an auditorium, all for the use of Westinghouse employees.

He established pension and benefit plans for his employees that continued after their deaths for their widows and orphans, another practice that was virtually unknown at the time. In 1903, a Relief Department was set up for disabled and ill workers. This was a model for the workers'-compensation programs that we have today.

Although many of his fellow industrialists complained that George Westinghouse was being much too generous, his employees were more than grateful. In recognition of his efforts on their behalf, a memorial to Westinghouse was built in Pittsburgh's Schenley Park in 1930—a memorial that was paid for with contributions from 55,000 Westinghouse employees.

More important, most of Westinghouse's achievements in the area of employee relations and benefits are common practice today. In the words of Samuel Gompers, founder of the American Federation of Labor: "If all employers of men treated their employees with the same consideration he does, the A.F. of L. would have to go out of existence."

Encouraging Inventive Minds

When his companies were faced with financial difficulties, one of the major bones of contention was the amount of money that George Westinghouse invested in research and development. Westinghouse was not motivated by money, though he certainly became a wealthy man. To him, money was something to be utilized—to be reinvested to do something good. The profit-minded managers saw this as a waste, but Westinghouse was convinced that ongoing research was essential to the success of his endeavors. This approach may have eventually caused him to lose control of his companies, but it is an important part of his legacy.

In 1888, what later became known as the Westinghouse Graduate Student Training Course was founded. Aware of the need to recruit new talent, Westinghouse sought out promising students and offered them training in engineering and a chance for employment once they had completed their training. That commitment to nurturing young minds was one of the inspirations for the Westinghouse Science Talent Search.

Established in 1942 and jointly sponsored by the Westinghouse Electric Corporation and the nonprofit Science Service, this program annually recognizes the work of the brightest science and math students in the United States. Every year, the coveted award means receiving not only recognition within the scientific community but also

The winners of the 1996 Westinghouse Science Talent Search.

scholarships for continuing education. Thus, the man whose own formal education ended in his teens is responsible for encouraging the continued education of scores of promising young people.

Since the program's beginnings, more than 110,000 students have submitted independent-research projects, and nearly $3 million in scholarships has been awarded. Each year, the top prize is a $40,000 scholarship; runners-up receive awards of $1,000 to $30,000, to be used for their education.

The program has certainly paid off for society as a whole. Five Nobel Prize winners have a "Westinghouse" in their past. Westinghouse finalists have also won the Fields Medal (the equivalent of a Nobel Prize in mathematics), the National Medal of Science, the MacArthur Foundation Fellowship, and election to the prestigious National Academy of Sciences and National Academy of Engineering. Of all the legacies George Westinghouse left us from the past, perhaps this is his greatest, for it is a gift to the future.

Glossary

alternating current (AC) A type of electric current in which the direction of current reverses itself (alternates) at regular intervals. Each change in direction is called a phase and is one half of a cycle. Normal household current is alternating current. Compare with *direct current.*

armature The part of a dynamo that rotates through a magnetic field to induce an electric current.

automatic brake (Westinghouse) A railroad brake that is set in the absence of air pressure and is released when air pressure is applied; a fail-safe brake.

block signal A railroad device that indicates whether a section of track (a block) is open for the passage of a train or whether another train or obstacle of some sort is in the block.

brake shoe A metal part that presses against a turning wheel, applying friction to slow and stop the wheel.

commutator A device attached to the armature of a dynamo that interferes with the reversal of current, thus changing alternating current to direct current.

converter A device attached to an induction motor that changes direct current to alternating current.

cycle One complete sequence of a recurring event. In alternating current, two phases, or reversals of current, equal one cycle.

direct current (DC) A type of electric current in which the flow does not reverse, remaining always in the same direction. Compare with alternating current.

dynamo A machine that produces electrical energy; a generator.

frog A section of rail that permits the wheels of a train to cross onto another, intersecting set of rails.

generator See *dynamo.*

hertz (Hz) A unit used to measure the frequency of alternating current. It is equal to one cycle per second.

hydraulic Operated by the pressure of water or another liquid.

hydroelectric Electrical power produced by generators run by the power of falling water.

induction Producing an electric charge in an object. Electromagnetic induction produces the charge by moving the object through a magnetic field.

interlocking signal A railroad signal connected to a track switch by a single mechanism so that the signal controls the opening and closing of the switch.

patent Legal protection to the inventor or discoverer of a new device, process, or composition of matter, or a new and useful improvement on an existing one. In the United States, a patent grants the exclusive right to the owner for 17 years.

phase A regularly occurring stage in a cycle. In alternating current, two phases (or reversals of current) equal a cycle.

pneumatic Operated by the pressure of air or another gas.

polyphase Having two or more phases. A polyphase motor produces a smooth flow of electric current through overlapping cycles.

reciprocating engine An engine whose driving force is a back-and-forth or up-and-down motion, as opposed to a circular, or rotary, motion.

rotary engine An engine whose driving force is a circular motion, usually caused by power pushing against vanes or blades attached to a central axis; also called a turbine.

step up/step down To increase/decrease the voltage of an electric current by means of a transformer.

straight-air brake (Westinghouse) A railroad brake that is set when air pressure is applied and is released when there is no air pressure.

transformer A device that increases or decreases voltage by passing a current from one coiled part to another in which the number of windings of the second coil differs from that of the first.

turbine See *rotary engine.*

voltage The force of an electric current.

Further Reading

Anderson, Kelly C. *Thomas Edison.* San Diego, CA: Lucent Books, 1994.

Ardley, Neil. *Light.* New York, Macmillan, 1992.

Catherall, Ed. *Exploring Electricity.* Austin, TX: Raintree Steck-Vaughn, 1990.

Coiley, Jack. *Train.* New York: Knopf, 1992.

Davies, Erle. *Inventions.* New York: Dorling Kindersley, 1995.

Dommermuth-Costa, Carol. *Nikola Tesla: A Spark of Genius.* Minneapolis, MN: Lerner, 1994.

George Westinghouse: 1846–1914. Pittsburgh: Westinghouse Electric Corp., 1986.

Haber, Louis. *Black Pioneers of Science and Invention.* New York: HarcourtBrace, 1992.

Hooper, Tony. *Electricity.* Austin, TX: Raintree Steck-Vaughn, 1993.

Jones, Charlotte Folts. *Mistakes That Worked.* New York: Doubleday, 1994.

Karnes, Frances A. and Bean, Suzanne M. *Girls and Young Women Inventing: 20 True Stories About Inventors and Their Inventions.* Minneapolis, MN: Free Spirit Publishing, 1995.
Machines and Inventions. New York: Time-Life Books, 1993.
Pollard, Michael. *The Lightbulb and How It Changed the World.* New York: Facts On File, 1995.
Scenes from a Great Life: George Westinghouse Centennial: 1846–1946. Pittsburgh: Westinghouse Electric Corporation.
Wormser, Richard. *The Iron Horse: How Railroads Changed America.* New York: Walker, 1993.

Sources

Asimov, Isaac. *Asimov's Biographical Encyclopedia of Science and Technology.* Garden City, NY: Doubleday, 1982.
———. *Asimov's Chronology of Science and Discovery.* New York: HarperCollins, 1994.
Baldwin, Neil. *Edison: Inventing the Century.* New York: Hyperion, 1995.
Burg, David F. *Chicago's White City of 1893.* Lexington, KY: University Press of Kentucky, 1976.
Cooke, David C. *Inventions That Made History.* New York: Putnam, 1968.
Daintith, John, Mitchell, Sarah, and Tootill, Elizabeth. *Biographical Encyclopedia of Scientists.* New York: Facts On File, 1981.
de Camp, L. Sprague. *The Heroic Age of American Invention.* Garden City, New York: Doubleday, 1961.
Derry, T. K., and Williams, Trevor. *A Short History of Technology.* New York: Oxford University Press, 1961.

Eyewitness Encyclopedia of Science. New York: Dorling Kindersley Multimedia, 1994. (CD-ROM)

Flatow, Ira. *They All Laughed: From Lightbulbs to Lasers, the Fascinating Stories Behind the Great Inventions That Changed Our Lives.* New York: HarperCollins, 1992.

Hall of Fame of Great Americans at NYU. New York: New York University Press, 1968.

Inventive Genius. Alexandria, VA: Time-Life Books, 1991.

Leupp, Francis E. *George Westinghouse: His Life and Achievements.* Boston: Little, Brown and Company, 1919.

Levine, I. E. *Inventive Wizard: George Westinghouse.* New York: Julian Messner, 1962.

Martin, Thomas Commerford. *The Inventions, Researches and Writings of Nikola Tesla.* New York: Barnes & Noble, 1995.

Meyer, Jerome S. *World Book of Great Inventions.* New York: World Publishers, 1956.

New Grolier Multimedia Encyclopedia. Danbury, CT: Grolier, 1993. (CD-ROM)

Pelletier, Paul A. *Prominent Scientists: An Index, 3rd ed.* New York: Neal-Schuman, 1994.

Prout, Henry G. *A Life of George Westinghouse.* New York: Charles Scribner's Sons, 1922.

Tesla, Nikola. *My Inventions: The Autobiography of Nikola Tesla.* Williston, VT: Hart Brothers, 1982.

United States Code, Title 35 [Patents], ch. 950, §101, §103. Washington, D.C.: United States Government Printing Office, 1989.

Vanderbilt, Byron M. *Inventing: How the Masters Did It.* Durham, NC: Moore, 1974.

Westinghouse Electric Corporation. *Centennial Review.* Pittsburgh: Westinghouse Electric Corporation, 1986.

———. *George Westinghouse: 1846–1914.* Pittsburgh: Westinghouse Electric Corporation, 1986.
———. *Scenes from a Great Life: George Westinghouse Centennial 1846–1946.* Pittsburgh: Westinghouse Electric Corporation, no date.
Westinghouse, George. "Broadening the Field of the Marine Steam Turbine," in *The Electric Journal*, January 1910, pp. 17–25.
———. "History of the Air Brake: Its Conception, Introduction and Development," Presidential Address, American Society of Mechanical Engineers, New York, December 6, 1910, reprinted in *The Electric Journa*l, December 1910, pp. 227–237.
Williams, T. L., ed. *A Biographical Dictionary of Scientists, 3rd ed.* New York: Wiley, 1982.

Index

Boldfaced, italicized numbers indicate picture references.

Photo Credits

Cover (background): ©Mike Mitchell/Photo Researchers, Inc.; cover (inset) and pages 4, 7, 11, 13, 23, 28–29, 34, 38, 40–41, 46–47, 62, 77, 80, 85, 93, 96, 102: Courtesy Westinghouse Electric Corporation; page 17: North Wind Picture Archives; pages 43, 59, 65, 83: Brown Brothers; page 74: National Portrait Gallery; page 91: Photodisc; page 98: ©F. Damm/Leo de Wys, Inc.
Graphics by Blackbirch Graphics, Inc.